TRUST ME,
I'M DR OZZY

TRUST ME, I'M DR OZZY

Advice from Rock's Ultimate Survivor

OZZY OSBOURNE

with Chris Ayres

sphere

SPHERE

First published in Great Britain in 2011 by Sphere

A CIP catalogue record for this book
is available from the British Library.

ISBN 978-1-84744-505-6

Typeset in Bembo by M Rules
Printed and bound in Great Britain by
Clays Ltd, St Ives plc

Papers used by Sphere are from well-managed forests
and other responsible sources.

MIX
Paper from
responsible sources
FSC
www.fsc.org   FSC® C104740

Sphere
An imprint of
Little, Brown Book Group
100 Victoria Embankment
London EC4Y 0DY

An Hachette UK Company
www.hachette.co.uk

www.littlebrown.co.uk

WARNING: OZZY OSBOURNE IS NOT A
QUALIFIED MEDICAL PROFESSIONAL

CAUTION IS ADVISED

SERIOUSLY, CAUTION IS ADVISED

Important Safety Information

(Hazardous) Contents

Dr Ozzy's Medicine Cabinet

Essential Items For All Patients

Description	Use(s)
Black Stuff, Greasy (From Dad's Shed)	Acne/Blemishes
Brandy (4 Bottles)	Hangover
Brick (1)	Various
Chicken (1, Alive)	Hangover (Severe)
Cocaine, Eighties-Vintage (Bag of)★	Athlete's Foot
Dynamite (2 Sticks)★	Constipation
Football (1, Leather)	Diagnostics
Lemon (1)	Common Cold
Sewing Kit (Stolen From Sister)	Surgery
Shotgun (1, Semi-Automatic)★	As Above
Snooker Cue (1)	Diagnostics
Stink Bombs (Novelty Pack of)	Indigestion (Severe)
Warm Chip Fat (Tub of)	Earache
Whiskey (2 Bottles)	Anything

★ Might not be legal where you live.

The Doctor is in ... *Sane*

A Note to All Patients

If someone had told me a few years ago that I'd end up writing a book of advice, I'd have punched them in the nose for taking the piss. I mean, unless the advice is how to end up dead or in jail, I'm not exactly qualified. I'm Ozzy Osbourne, not Oprah fucking Winfrey.

But here I am: 'Dr Ozzy', as people call me now. And to be *totally* honest with you – I love this new gig.

I suppose it all started just before my last world tour, when a bloke from the *Sunday Times Magazine* in London came over to my house and asked if I wanted to be their new 'health and relationship' columnist. When I'd finished spitting out tea over my Yorkshire terrier, I asked him, 'Are you *sure* you've got the right person?' He said yeah, they were sure. If I wanted the job, the guy added, readers would write in with their problems – everything from stubbed toes, to tearaway kids, to fallouts with the in-laws – and I'd give my answers. I wouldn't even have to put pen to paper: someone would call me up every week so I could dictate my words of wisdom over the telephone.

'Look – are you *absolutely one hundred per cent sure* you've got the right person?' I asked him again.

He just smiled.

The funny thing is, the more I thought about it, the more it made sense . . . in a crazy kind of way. I mean, by all accounts, I'm a medical miracle. It's all very well going on a bender for a couple of weeks, but mine went on for the best part of forty years. At one point I was knocking back four bottles of cognac a day, blacking out, coming round, and starting again. Meanwhile, during the filming of *The Osbournes*, I was shoving forty-two different types of prescription medication down my neck every single day. Each of those drugs had about twenty or thirty different side-effects, so there were about a thousand things wrong with me at any one time, just thanks to the pills. And that was before the dope I was smoking in my 'safe room', away from the cameras; or the crates of beer I was putting away; or the speed I was doing before my daily jogs around Beverly Hills. I also used to get through cigars like they were cigarettes. I'd smoke 'em in bed. '*Do you mind?*' I'd ask Sharon, as I lit up a Cuban the size of the *Red October*. 'Please, go ahead,' she'd say – before whacking me with a copy of *Vanity Fair*.

Of course, I've also taken a few, well, not-exactly-legal things in my time. There are probably rats in US Army labs who've seen fewer chemicals than I have. It's amazing that none of that dodgy shit ever killed me. On the other hand, maybe it shouldn't be such a surprise, given all the other things I've survived: like being hit by a plane (it crashed into my tour bus when I was asleep with Sharon in the back); or getting a false-positive HIV test (my immune system had been knocked out by booze and cocaine, not the virus); or a suspected rabies infection (after eating a bat); or being told that I had Parkinson's disease (it was actually a rare genetic tremor). I was even put in the loony bin for a while. 'Do you masturbate, Mr Osbourne?' was the first thing the guy in the white coat asked me. 'I'm here for my head, not my dick!' I told him.

Oh, yeah, and I've been dead twice. That happened (so I'm told) while I was in a chemically induced coma after I broke my neck in a quad-bike accident. I've got more metal screws in me now than an IKEA flatpack – all thanks to the amazing doctors and nurses of the NHS.

I always used to say that when I die, I should donate my body to the Natural History Museum. But since accepting the job as the *Sunday Times*' Dr Ozzy – which snowballed into a gig at *Rolling Stone*, too – I don't have to any more, 'cos a bunch of scientists from Harvard University offered to take a sample of my DNA and map out my entire 'human genome'. 'What d'you wanna do *that* for?' I asked them. 'To find out why you're still alive,' they said. Thanks to them, I now know for sure that I'm a 'genetic anomaly' – or at least that's what they told a room full of mega-brains at TEDMED, a medical conference in San Diego, when they announced the results in 2010 (see Chapter Seven).

The fact that I'm still alive isn't the only reason why I agreed to become Dr Ozzy, though. I've seen literally *hundreds* of doctors and shrinks during my lifetime – and have spent well over a million quid on them – so I'm now convinced that I know more about being a doctor than some doctors do. And that's not just 'cos of the insane lifestyle I've led – I'm also a terrible hypochondriac. I'll catch a disease off the telly, me. Being ill is like a hobby. I've even started to diagnose my own diseases with the help of the

Internet. (Actually, my assistant Tony does all the research for me, 'cos I ain't exactly Stephen fucking Hawking when it comes to using a computer.)

Of course, I'm always asked: 'If you're such a hypochondriac, Ozzy, how could you have taken all those drugs over the years?' But the thing is, when you have an addictive personality, you never think anything bad's gonna happen. It's like, 'Oh, well, I didn't do as much so-and-so/didn't drink as much as him/didn't do as much coke as he did, etc., etc.' Now, that might be fine in theory, but in my case the 'so-and-so' in question was usually a certified lunatic like John Bonham or, even worse, Mel Gibson. Which meant they'd put enough up their noses to blast off into outer fucking space.

Another thing I'd always tell myself was: 'Oh, a doctor gave me the drugs, and he *must* know what he's doing.' But that ignored the fact that I'd then administer the stuff myself, usually at five hundred times the recommended dosage.

It's a miracle I didn't end up like Michael Jackson, or any number of other tragic rock'n'roll cases. In fact, my friends knew me as 'Dr Ozzy' for years before I started giving advice professionally, 'cos I was like a walking pharmacy. I remember in the 1980s, a good mate of mine came to me for help with his leg ache, so I went to get my 'special suitcase', pulled out a pill, and said, 'Here, take one of these.' It was only ibuprofen, but these were the days before you could buy it over-the-counter in Britain. He came back a few hours later and said, 'Wow! Dr Ozzy, you cured me!' The only problem was that the pill was the size of a golf ball – big enough to cure an elephant. The poor bloke didn't shit or sleep for two months.

He didn't thank me so much for *that*.

But I've given more than just medication to my friends. As insane as it sounds, a lot of people have come to me for family advice. I suppose it's 'cos they saw me raising Jack and Kelly during *The Osbournes*, so they think I'm like Bill Cosby or something. They ask me stuff like 'How do I get my kids to have safe sex?' or 'How do I talk to them about drugs?' I'm happy to help whenever I can. The only trouble is, when I talked to *my* kids about drugs, the conversation went along the lines of 'Where's your stash?' and 'Can I have some, please?'

I've become a better father since then. After all, during the worst days of my addiction, I wasn't really a father at all, I was just another one of Sharon's kids. But I'm a different person now: I don't smoke, I don't drink, I don't get high – unless you count endorphins from the jogging machine. Which means I enjoy my family more than ever: not just my five amazing kids (two of them to my first wife), but now my five grandkids. Plus, after thirty years, my marriage to Sharon is stronger than ever.

So I must be doing *something* right.

When you live full time in Los Angeles, as I've done for the past few years, you often feel that people spend so much time trying to save their lives that they forget to *live* them. I mean, at the end of the day, we're all going to die, one way or another. So why kill yourself with worry?

For me, though, the decision to change my life wasn't really about my health. It was about the fact that I wasn't having fun any more. As I used to say, I'd put the 'wreck' into recreation. I was on Ambien, Klonopin, temazepam, chloral hydrate, alcohol, Percocet, codeine – and that was just on my days off! But morphine was my favourite. I didn't do it for very long, mind you. Sharon would find me passed out on the kitchen floor with the dog licking my forehead, and she put a stop to it. And thank God she did: I'd have kicked the bucket a long time ago otherwise.

But it was tobacco that really put me over the edge. I'm a singer, that's how I earn a living, but I'd get a sore throat, then cough my way through a pack of Marlboro full-strength, to the point where I had to cancel gigs. It was ridiculous – the stupidest fucking habit you could ever imagine. So cigarettes were the first thing I quit, and that started the ball rolling. Now I take drugs only for *real* problems, like high cholesterol and heartburn.

I can sort of understand if people think it's more rock 'n'roll to die young. But what really winds me up is when you hear, 'Oh, my great Aunt Nelly smoked eighty fags a day and drank sixteen pints of Guinness before going to bed every night, and she lived to a hundred and three.' Okay, yeah, that can happen. My own gran lived to ninety-nine. But the odds ain't exactly on your side. Especially once you've reached the age of sixty-two, like me.

Another thing that drvies me fucking mental is people who never get check-ups and never go to the doctor, even when they're half-dead. It ain't macho – it's fucking pathetic. I had my prostate checked just the other week, for example, 'cos I'm on a three-year plan for prostate and colon tests. I couldn't believe how many of my male friends said, 'Your prostate? What's *that*?'

I was like, 'Look, women get breast cancer, and blokes get cancer of the prostate.'

One guy even asked me, 'Where is it?'

I told him, 'Up your arse,' and he went, 'So how do they check that, then?'

I said, 'How do you *think* they check it? It starts with a rubber glove and ends with your voice rising ten octaves.'

My prostate guy here in California says that every man over the age of fifty will develop some kind of prostate problem as he gets older, but only half will get tested. Yet nowadays you can cure prostate cancer, no problem at all, if you spot it early enough. It's the same with colon cancer. Don't get me wrong: I'm the first to admit that the preparation for the colon cancer test ain't exactly glamorous. They give you this horrendous liquid to drink, then you have to crap through the eye of a needle until your backside is so clean that if you open your mouth, you can see daylight at the other end. But it's only 'cos I got tested for colon cancer that my wife did the same ... and her test came back positive. Thanks to that, they caught it in time, and she's alive today. That's a huge deal.

So when I first became Dr Ozzy, my first message was: 'Don't be ignorant!' To men, in particular, I wanted to say: 'Don't think a doctor's never put his finger up a bloke's ass before. They do it every day, so get over yourself.' Besides, what would you rather have, a strange man's finger up your arse on a Monday morning or the sound of a pine box being nailed shut over your head?

Having said that, every case is different, which I realised very quickly when I became Dr Ozzy. For example, after reassuring my readers that they had nothing to fear from dropping their trousers in front of their GP, I received an e-mail from a guy called Geoff in London. He wrote:

Dear Dr Ozzy:
After hurting my rear end end while squatting down to tile a floor, I asked my GP to take a look at it. He umm'ed-and-ahh'ed for a while, then sent me off to a local teaching hospital, where a very excited specialist said he needed to perform an examination. After giving

me one of those back-to-front robes to wear, he lay me down on a slab on my side, and proceeded to round up some 20 junior doctors, who then took turns to file past my exposed behind, scribbling notes and snapping photographs as they went. Their verdict after what seemed like ten lifetimes? I had a rare 'perianal haematoma' . . . which would go away by itself.

All I can say is: sorry, Geoff. If it's any consolation, I once mooned a crowd of about half a million people at a gig, so you certainly don't hold the world record for having the largest number of people gazing up your asshole. That one belongs to *me*.

To be honest, I can still hardly believe the stuff people write to me about. One guy asked if he should cut down on his cocaine use . . . 'cos he'd just found out that he had high cholesterol. Another time, a girl in America – she was twenty-two – asked if it was okay to sleep with her mum's (younger) boyfriend, or if that would make things weird at family get-togethers. I mean, what is *wrong* with these people? And, as you'll see when you read on, that ain't the half of it. Sometimes even Dr Ozzy is lost for words.

When it comes to routine stuff, though, I pretty much always know the right answers. That's the thing about being a worrier, especially a worrier who's a hypochondriac: you end up investigating every last ache and twinge, so, over time, all these random facts end up sticking in your head. If only I could remember lyrics so easily.

I wasn't always such a hypochondriac, mind you. When I was growing up in Aston, our family GP was a guy called Dr Rosenfield, and I'd do anything to get out of an appointment with him – mainly 'cos his receptionist was a woman with a full-on beard. I ain't kidding you: a big, black, bushy beard. It freaked me out. She was like Captain Pugwash in a frock. And Dr Rosenfield's surgery was so gloomy, you felt worse coming out of that place than you did when you went in. As for Dr Rosenfield himself, he wasn't a bad guy, but he wasn't exactly comforting, either. I remember falling out of a tree one time when I was scrumping apples: I hit a branch on the way down, and my eye swelled up like a big black balloon. When I got home, my old man smacked me around the ear before sending me off to get my injury looked at. Then Dr Rosenfield smacked me around the other ear. I couldn't believe it.

I rarely received any proper medical care in those days. If one of the six Osbourne kids had an earache, they'd get a spoonful of hot chip fat down their earhole. That was the done thing. And my gran would give us milk and mutton fat for a croupy cough. As for my father, he had a tin of stuff in his shed – I don't know what it was, but it was black and greasy. If you got a boil on your neck, he'd go, 'I'll get rid of that for you, son, heh-heh-heh,' and slap it on. You'd scream, 'NOT THE BLACK TIN! NOOO!' but that was all my folks could afford. Shelling out on zit cream from the chemist was never gonna happen when they could barely afford to put food on the table.

My father was one of those people who'd never see a doctor. He'd never take a day off work at the factory, either. He'd literally have to be missing a limb to call in sick – even then, he'd probably just hop to the factory, like nothing had happened. I don't think he got a single check-up, right until the end of his life – by then, he was riddled with cancer. His prostate gave up first, though. I don't know why he avoided doctors – it was all free on the NHS – but it made me think the opposite way. My logic is: if I go to the doctor now, and there's something wrong with me, they'll catch it, so I'll get to live another day. Don't get me wrong: I ain't afraid of dying. Although it would be good to know *where* it's gonna happen, so I could avoid going there . . .

Sometimes I think people in Britain don't make enough use of the NHS, because they're too busy complaining about it. Americans – who'll queue outside a sports arena for three days just to go to a free clinic – can't believe the deal we Brits get. I'll never forget the first time I got an X-ray done in the States after my quad-bike crash. The doc came into the room, holding up my slide and whistling through his teeth. 'How much did all that cost you, huh?' he asked, pointing to all the rods and bolts holding together my neck and back. 'A couple of mill? Three? Four? Are you still getting the bills?'

'Actually, it was free,' I told him. 'I had the accident in England.'

I almost had to call for a nurse, he got such a shock.

If you're a celebrity, mind you, medical care in America is incredible. Too much so, if you're an addict, because they'll hand out pills like you're in a shopping mall. Whenever I do a gig in the US, I'll always have a doctor check me out before the show, and in the bad old days I used to score just about anything I wanted off those guys. At one point, I basically bought my own doctor and installed him in my house. It was magic until Sharon got wind of it. In England, I used to have to make up a back-ache, or hit myself over the head with a lump of wood to get my hands on a Vicodin. In America, I just had to say the word. It stopped only when the doctors realised that they had to answer to the Voice of God – Sharon.

'If you give him one more dodgy pill, *you'll* be the one who needs a doctor,' she'd say.

To be fair to the American doctors, they do come up with some mind-blowing technology. For example, I just had my eyes fixed with Crystalens surgery. My vision was so bad it was starting to give me problems on stage. So they took out my natural lenses – which were all fogged up by cataracts – and replaced them with bionic ones, which can focus by themselves. Left eye first, then the right a week later. It's amazing. Just unbelievable. No pain, for starters. And I can read again. I can see over there, over here, it's fucking incredible. I've no idea how much it cost – probably eight tours, or something – but it's totally changed my life.

I'm a new man in so many ways. I might be sixty-two, but I haven't felt so young since the 1960s. Aside from my eyes, the other big change in my life is that I've pretty much become a vegetarian. Seriously. It's my new phase: brown rice and vegetables. I don't even drink milk, apart from a splash in my tea. And, no, it ain't because of the *animals*. I mean, I used to work in a slaughterhouse, killing two hundred cows a day. I once ate a bat, for fuck's sake. So you won't see me marching over the frozen tundra, hunting down seal-clubbers. It's just that I can't digest meat any more. I finally gave it up a few weeks ago, after I went out for a steak with my friend Zakk Wylde. I might as well have sealed my arse with cement, 'cos I couldn't crap for a week. I love the taste of beef, but it ain't worth it.

I ain't into any of that organic bollocks, either. People think they're buying another day on this earth when they pay for that stuff, so they get ripped off. If you want organic, grow your own, man. I used to when I was married to my first wife and we had a little cottage in Ranton, Staffordshire. A veggie patch also happens to be a great place to hide your stash of drugs. Having said that, I'd always get stoned and forget where I'd buried the stuff. I once spent a whole week at the bottom of the garden, trying to find a lump of Afghan hash. The missus thought I was just really worried about my carrots.

I suppose when people hear stories like that, they might think I'm too much of a bad example to give advice. I wouldn't argue – and I'd hate for anyone to think, Oh, if Ozzy survived all of that outrageous behaviour, so can I. But you know what? If people can learn from my stupid shit without having to repeat any of it, or if they can take some comfort from the crazy, fucked-up things my family has been through over the years, or if just hearing me talk about colonoscopies makes them less embarrassed about getting tested for colon cancer, that's more than enough for me. Dr Ozzy's job will be done.

One last thing. Being a hypochondriac, I would *never* tell someone just to stop worrying and come back later if the symptoms get any worse. That's bollocks, in my book. As I've always warned my own doctors: 'One day, you're gonna be standing at my graveside, and while the priest is reading out the eulogy, you're gonna look down at the inscription on my headstone. And it's gonna say: *See? I told you I was fucking ill!*'

TRUST ME,
I'M DR OZZY

1

How to Cure (Almost) Anything

You'll Never Be Ill Again . . . Probably

If there's one thing I've learned as Dr Ozzy, it's that everyone wants to be cured immediately . . . or, better yet, three days ago. Luckily for the people who come to me with their problems, I'm exactly the same. I mean, why go to all the trouble of a low-carb diet if you can get rid of your gut with a needle and a suction pump? Why take it easy after an injury when you can pop a few painkillers and carry on?

As far as I can tell, there's only one drawback to quick fixes: *they don't fucking work*. Either that or they sort out whatever's bothering you, but create another ten problems along the way. Take sleeping pills. For years, I had trouble getting any shut-eye, so I started using a popular brand of sleeping medication. Before I knew it, I'd forgotten everything since 1975. The trouble was, my body built up an immunity to the drugs so quickly that I ended up necking a whole jar of the stuff just to get five minutes' rest. That was when my memory blackouts started, along with a bunch of other crazy side-effects, like wandering around the house stark naked at two in the morning.

What I should have done was find out *why* I wasn't sleeping. Go after the cause, not the symptom, and figure out what was making me anxious. But it's human nature, isn't it? We're all tempted by the cheap 'n' easy bodge job, even though we know it ain't gonna last. That's why I've dedicated this chapter to 'instant' cures: urban myths, old wives' tales and bizarre stories I've picked up on the road. Some of them have worked for me in the past. Others are bollocks. I'll let you decide which is which.

> **Dear Dr Ozzy:**
> **What's the best cure for a hangover, in your (considerable) experience?**
> **Justin, London**

This is an easy one: have another pint. You'll be feeling much better in no time. It took me forty years of trying everything and anything to make the morning after feel better – short of actually giving up booze – until I finally realised that the only thing that ever worked was just to get pissed again. Like a lot of things, it was obvious in hindsight.

> **Dear Dr Ozzy:**
> **Help! I've got a cold. How can I get rid of it ASAP?**
> **Tony, Boston**

Funnily enough, getting pissed is also a great cure for the common cold. For example, I used to have this magic recipe for a 'Hot Ozzy' (as I used to call it). You take two pints of whiskey, boil it up on the stove, add a bit of lemon — it's very important, the lemon — then drink it as quickly as you can. Trust me, by the time you've downed a Hot Ozzy, you won't just have forgotten you're ill — you'll have forgotten your own name.

Dear Dr Ozzy:
I've been told that the easiest way to treat athlete's foot is to pee on your toes, because the chemical in anti-fungal cream (urea) can also be found in urine. Does this work?
Pierre, Ipswich

I don't know. Back in the eighties, though, I used to deal with athlete's foot by pouring cocaine on my toes. They cut the stuff with so much foot powder in those days, it was the best treatment you could find if you had an outbreak on the road, away from your local chemist's. The only problem was the price: about three grand a toe. If I'd known about the peeing thing, I might have saved myself a fortune.

Dear Dr Ozzy:
What's the best way to get over jet-lag quickly?
James, Toronto

They say you should line the insides of your shoes with brown paper during the flight. Unfortunately, like a lot of things people say, that's bollocks. In reality, there's only thing that'll stop your body clock getting messed up, and it's called staying at fucking home.

Dear Dr Ozzy:
What's the best cure for 'seasonal affective disorder'? I

get incredibly depressed every year before the clocks
go forward, but I can't afford to move to the Florida
Keys.
Felicity, Doncaster

All you need is a bit of heat and light. If you can't afford a
plane ticket, I'm not sure what to suggest, apart from set-
ting your house on fire – which obviously ain't a very
clever idea.

Dear Dr Ozzy:
A doctor in Italy says he can cure cancer patients by
giving them baking soda. What's your opinion?
Chris (no address given)

A friend of mine got cancer a few years ago and didn't want
to go through any of the conventional treatments, so he
spent months doing all the dead cat voodoo stuff – and now
the poor bloke's dead. Obviously, I ain't gonna criticise
anyone in that position, 'cos if you've been told you've only
got weeks to live, you're gonna do whatever you think you
need to do. But baking soda? You're fixing a tumour, not
a cupcake. Also, if it really worked, wouldn't baking soda
be in short supply by now? Personally, my rule of thumb is
that if some wacky new treatment sounds too good to be
true, it is.

Dear Dr Ozzy:
According to my great aunt, nine white raisins, soaked
in one tablespoon of gin for two weeks, will get rid of
arthritis. Is this right?
Phil, Luton

The Osbourne family has the same recipe, passed down through the generations. In our version, though, there's only one white raisin, and it's soaked in nine bottles of gin, for two minutes. It's great for pretty much anything.

DR OZZY'S AMAZING MEDICAL MISCELLANY

Crazy Cures Through the Ages

➕ In Egypt, they reckon that being buried in the sand during the hottest part of the day can cure rheumatism, joint pain and impotence. If you stay out there long enough without water, it can also cure being alive.

➕ To treat a stuttering child, Chinese doctors used to recommend smacking the kid in the face – but only on a cloudy day. If anyone ever tried that on me, they'd get a knee in the balls, n-n-n-n-no matter what the fucking weather was.

➕ The only anaesthetic in medieval England was a potion made up of lettuce juice, gall from a castrated boar, briony, opium, hemlock juice, vinegar and what passed for wine in those days. I'm pretty sure I had exactly the same cocktail in Miami while on the road with Mötley Crüe in 1984.

Dear Dr Ozzy:
Have you ever suffered from heartburn, or acid indigestion? If so, what do you do about it?
Joan, Shropshire

Oh, I used to get it all the time. I'd wake up at three in the morning with a horrendous burning sensation in my chest. Then, one night my bed caught fire, and I realised I'd been going to sleep every night with a lit cigarette in my hand. When I stopped doing that, the problem went away.

> Dear Dr Ozzy:
> Please help me – I can't stop scratching my testicles at night! It's getting so bad, my wife is threatening to sleep in another room. And now I've noticed a red rash, which seems to be spreading to my wider nether regions. Is this 'jock itch'?
> Ted, Northumberland

Sounds like it to me. The first thing to do is change your underwear. Personally, I find that nylon Y-fronts give me a raging case of ball itch: it's like they're on fire, man. Now, I wouldn't mention this to your missus (if you ever want her to go near you again), but it's all to do with trapped sweat. So the next thing to do is get yourself some anti-fungal cream – the same stuff you'd use for athlete's foot – and it should calm down in a few days.

> Dear Dr Ozzy:
> Thanks to your medical wisdom, I already know your cure for a cold – a Hot Ozzy – but what's the best way to prevent one?
> Lucy, Bristol

Your local chemist's will sell you any old bollocks to 'prevent' a cold – they must make a fortune during virus season – but really you've just gotta ride it out. There's no harm in having a Hot Ozzy or two as a precaution, though.

If it does nothing else, it'll make your day at work go by a lot faster.

Dear Dr Ozzy:
What's the most effective treatment for hiccups?
Lauren, Carlisle

Extreme pain, combined with the element of surprise.

DR OZZY'S INSANE-BUT-TRUE STORIES

The 430 Million Hiccup Man

➕ The longest-ever attack of hiccups went on for sixty-eight years – *sixty-eight* fucking years, man! – and was suffered by an American guy named Charles Osborne (no relation). It started in 1922, when he was weighing a hog for slaughter in Iowa, and didn't end until 1990. The worst thing is, he dropped dead from an ulcer only a year after the hiccups stopped. There was some good news, though. The hiccups didn't prevent Charles from getting on with his life: he managed to get hitched and have five kids (which proves that anyone can get their end away, if they put their mind to it). He was even mentioned in the *Guinness Book of Records* and Trivial Pursuit. Apparently, Charles hiccupped forty times a minute in the early days but slowed to 'only' twenty times a minute as he got older. In total, they reckon he suffered 430 million hiccups over his entire life. It's a good job I never sat next to the guy on a plane – I'd have pushed him out of the emergency exit after five fucking minutes.

> Dear Dr Ozzy:
> What's the best cure for snoring? I need something to shut up my husband, who sounds like a whale with a foghorn stuck in its throat, before I kick him downstairs to the sofa.
> Jane, Acton

I used to share a room with a guy who had the worst snore in the world, I swear. One night, I got so fed up with him, I filled a wastepaper basket with water, put it next to his bed, and told him, 'One snore, and it's going over your head.' And you know what? It cured him. Or at least he didn't dare go to sleep until he was pretty fucking sure I'd already nodded off. Having said that, I'm a terrible snorer myself. So is Sharon. Our seventeen dogs snore, too. When all of us are in action at the same time, our bedroom must sound like the London Nostril Choir. It's never bothered me, though. I'm usually asleep.

> Dear Dr Ozzy:
> Is it really true that chicken soup can help with congestion?
> Rita, Germany

Yes — especially if you add a pint of unleaded petrol. Seriously, though, I've definitely heard that there's a chemical in chicken soup that breaks up all the gunk in your nose, making you breathe a bit easier. But in my experience it only lasts for as long as you're eating the stuff. It's more likely the heat of the soup that gets the old snot running.

> Dear Dr Ozzy:
> What's the best cure for depression?
> 'Peter', County Armagh

It's tempting to give you a funny response to this, but unfortunately depression ain't funny. I should know – I've suffered from it myself. I recommend you do what I did – talk to your GP. My doc prescribed a low dose of an anti-depressant called Zoloft (also known as sertraline), and it does the job. Of course, you hear a lot of people saying that anti-depressants just put a sticking plaster on the problem, instead of solving the real cause. They might have a point ... but it's very easy to say that *if you ain't fucking depressed*. The only big problem I've got with anti-depressants is that they ended my sex life. Trying to get down to some action these days is like trying to raise the *Titanic*. It would be depressing ... if I weren't on anti-depressants. As it is, I don't give a flying one.

Dear Dr Ozzy:
Is it true that 'onion syrup' – onions cooked with brown sugar or honey – can help cure a cough?
Jamie, Madrid

No idea. I *do* know that if you eat enough onions, it'll cure people from wanting to speak to you.

Chapter Notes:
How To Cure (Almost) Anything
(Cut Out and Keep)

	Severe headache	Sudden, excruciating bowel pain	Baldness	Stiff neck	Blurred vision
First thing to ask yourself	Have I been listening to Radio 4? *And/or...* Did I drive my car into a stationary object?	What's the waddling distance to the nearest toilet? *And/or...* Why did I wear white trousers today?	If I shave all my hair off, will I look like Bruce Willis ... or an axe murderer?	Do I have a Viagra pill stuck in my throat?	Am I underwater? *And/or...* Was the tenth pint *really* necessary?
Quick fix	Shoot the radio *And/or...* Massage forehead with the airbag	Unclench buttocks, prepare for the consequences	Cover bare patches with spray paint *And/or...* Make wig out of an old beer mat	Picture Simon Cowell in a miniskirt (should relieve any swelling)	Do what the officer says and get out of the fountain, 'cos you're fucking nicked
What *not* to say to your doctor later	Is a brain transplant expensive?	D'you mind if I use your shitter? I may be some time	Tell me, Doc: how did *you* feel when you turned into a slaphead?	When I imagined Simon Cowell in a miniskirt, my neck got even stiffer	I think beer gives me astigmatism

Dr Ozzy's Trivia Quiz:
Magic Medicines

*Find the answers – and add up
your score – on page 277*

1. **Which musical instrument allegedly cures 'sleep apnoea' (when you don't breathe properly at night)?**

a) A kazoo

b) A didgeridoo

c) An Auto-Tune machine

2. **What the fuck is 'Peruvian Viagra'?**

a) A squashed frog

b) A well-trained hamster

c) A rare type of bean

3. **The ancient Egyptians treated blindness with . . .**

a) Tickling

b) Sunlight

c) Bat's blood

4. Which 'cure' for AIDS has actually helped spread the disease?

a) Bonking a virgin
b) Putting the condom on your big toe
c) Smothering your private parts in clarified butter

5. In the 1960s, psychiatrists treated alcoholics with ...

a) Alcohol
b) LSD
c) Hospital-grade laxatives

2

Have a Fucking Egg

The Truth About Diet & Exercise

One of the saddest questions I've ever been asked as Dr Ozzy came from a middle-aged woman in Worcester – Sally, her name was – who wanted to know if it was safe to 'Go to work on an egg' (as the old ad slogan used to say). Someone had told her that yolk was bad news, so she was considering a switch to low-fat bean curd or some bullshit. I could hardly believe it, man. This woman was old enough to remember when it was considered perfectly acceptable to fry bread in lard, or let kids breathe fumes from leaded petrol. Yet she'd convinced herself that one boiled egg was gonna send her to an early grave. I mean, *really*? That's how crazy things are now.

The trouble is, it's so easy to get everything out of proportion. I'm guilty of the same thing myself. For example, I recently went through a phase of having egg-white omelettes for lunch as part of a low-calorie diet. Then one day this light bulb went off in my head, and I thought, You know what? *This tastes like fucking shit.* So I went back to eating normal omelettes and, low and behold, I *didn't* grow five extra bellies overnight. As long as you're not having a dozen eggs every morning, another dozen for lunch, and another dozen for dinner, what's the problem? It the same with anything else: all you need is a bit of common sense and you'll be fine.★

Having said that, common sense has never exactly been one of my fortes. Because of my addictive personality, I tend to do anything and everything to excess. Like when I gave up McDonald's and switched to Mexican fast food – within twenty-four hours, I was addicted to fucking burritos. Or when I gave up being a lazy bastard and started to exercise – I was soon taking a gram of speed so I could run around the block faster. Trying to live the perfect balanced lifestyle is a never-ending struggle if you're as unbalanced as I am. As a matter of fact, I think it's hard for everyone, insane or otherwise. But as I always say to people, you should never stop trying. Just take every new day as it comes – and go easy on the triple-decker bacon chilli cheeseburgers.

> **Dear Dr Ozzy:**
> My daughter announced today that she's going on the 'Five Bite Diet'. She can drink whatever she wants (if it has no calories) but has only five bites of lunch and five bites of dinner. As a precaution, she's also taking a multi-vitamin tablet every day. Should I try and stop her?
> Julie, Sunderland

★ Before anyone gives me a bollocking, talk to your doc about your diet if you have high cholesterol.

I've never heard of this before, but it doesn't surprise me that it exists. In fact, I tried a similar kind of extreme diet myself once – I called it the 'Walking Corpse' diet, 'cos it made you feel like the living dead. And, of course, five seconds after I stopped, I put back on all the weight I'd lost. I mean, I honestly don't know what to tell you when it comes to dieting, 'cos I came to the conclusion a long time ago that nothing works apart from eating healthier and eating *less*, full stop. Catchy-sounding quick fixes are usually good for only one thing: making a shitload of dough for the person who came up with the idea. Bearing in mind that your daughter will probably do the opposite of whatever you tell her, just suggest that she gets the advice of her GP before she starts sniffing her dinner instead of eating it. That's the best way to make sure she doesn't do anything dangerous.

Dear Dr Ozzy:
My doctor has told me that I have high cholesterol.
Does that mean I should stop taking cocaine?
Andrew, Los Angeles

Hang on a fucking minute! Don't you think you're putting the cart before the horse a bit here? I suppose you're thinking that because the cholesterol gives you a higher risk of a heart attack, the coke might push you over the edge. But you shouldn't be doing cocaine, full stop. It doesn't matter if you've got high cholesterol, low blood sugar, a gammy leg or a runny nose. It's like a forty-a-day smoker asking if he should move out of the city to get some fresh air. Where's the logic, man? Here's the thing with coke: you can drop dead from it *instantly*, 'cos you're buying it on the street, so you never know what the fuck's gonna be in it. It also messes with your head, makes you say stupid things, and can land you in prison. So if you keep taking the coke, you can forget all about your cholesterol – the chances are you'll be dead long before you need to start worrying about hardened arteries.

Dear Dr Ozzy:
I can't stop drinking Coca-Cola. Do you think I've become addicted to the caffeine?
David, Staffordshire

I know plenty of people who are addicted to cola – and not just the brand-name stuff, but the big, cheap gallon bottles you get in a supermarket. It's not so much the caffeine they get hooked on, though – it's the *sugar*. Try switching to a diet brand. Or better yet, have a good old cuppa instead.

Dear Dr Ozzy:
My boyfriend goes swimming six times a week and does yoga twice a week, but he's still getting fat. Why?
Eve, Ireland

There's only one explanation: he's eating sandwiches between lengths. Either that or he's lying to you about the exercise. I recommend hiring a private detective to follow him around for a week.

Dear Dr Ozzy:
Is it really true that you're a vegetarian now? Have you bitten the head off a lettuce yet?
Paul, Derby

Very funny. I'd say I'm *borderline* vegetarian now, 'cos I find it hard to digest red meat. When I'm at home in LA, the woman who works for me – she's Ethiopian – cooks veggies on the barbeque with brown rice. It's spicy, not boring at all, and there's nothing like a good old curry to unplug a clogged sixty-two-year-old arsehole. Mind you, it's hard to keep it up when I'm on the road, 'cos you can't always get hold of healthy food when you're so far away from home. Eventually, though, you lose your tolerance for meat altogether, so maybe I'll have no choice. I remember one time in 1968 when one of my old bandmates from Black Sabbath, Terence 'Geezer' Butler – the first vegetarian I'd ever met – ate a hot dog in Belgium 'cos he was broke and starving, and it was the only thing he could scrounge that day. The poor bloke was in hospital a few hours later. In fact, I don't think he took another shit until 1983.

Dear Dr Ozzy:
Is there any truth in the claim that food colouring –
which they used to make out of coal-tar – makes kids
hyperactive? Or is this just another of those trendy
myths?
Erica, Los Angeles

When I was growing up, no one cared about what was in their food – calories, preservatives, colouring, or otherwise. We just ate what was on the table, 'cos the alternative was a smack round the ear and going to bed hungry. And I have to say, looking back, we were all fucking *nuts*. I mean, it's hard to imagine a more hyperactive kid than me: I spent half the day bouncing off the walls, and the other half bouncing on my bed. Was it the E-numbers? Who knows, man. In a perfect world, we'd all grow our own food. But you can't exactly grow a fish finger or a can of beans, can you? So my advice is just be careful and make sure that your kids are eating plenty of fruit and veggies.

DR OZZY'S INCREDIBLY HELPFUL TIPS

Diet – Things to Avoid

- If you're trying to stay slim, it ain't a good idea to take part in Nathan's Famous Hot Dog Eating Contest, held every year in New York. The last record-breaking winner scoffed 66 hot dogs – that's 19,600 calories – in 12 minutes. A few hours later, he broke another record for the amount of time he spent on the shitter.

- I've suffered the consequences of a few dodgy curries in my time, but nothing comes close to eating a badly cooked fugu ('river pig') in Japan. The fish contains tetrodotoxin, which paralyses your muscles and stops your breathing within twenty-four hours. There ain't no antidote, either. So, if you get poisoned, it'll be the worst – and last – day of your life.

- Fast food has always been a guilty pleasure for me, but if there's one thing you should probably steer clear of, it's the '100×100' burger at the In-N-Out chain in America (you have to special order it). It consists of 100 beef patties and 100 slices of cheese, and costs about $100. That doesn't include the price of the ambulance you'll need after eating it, though.

- If you go to Sardinia on holiday, don't *ever* order 'Casu Marzu'. It's basically a sheep's milk cheese, but it's infested with *live* insect larvae, which look like wriggly little white worms. I ain't fucking kidding you. The worst part is that the worms jump up and down, so you've gotta put your hand over the plate while you're eating – otherwise you get 'em in your eyes and up your nose.

Dear Dr Ozzy:
I like to drink beer, but I'm getting fat. I hate to think I might have to give up booze just to stay in shape. Is there an alternative to beer that has fewer calories?
Miles, Kailua, Hawaii

Not in Hawaii, there ain't. It's all Mai Tais, Zombies and Hoola-tinis. There's enough fruit juice and syrup and fuck knows what else in those things to give you three extra chins in the time it takes to drink one. The thing is, you can't have it both ways: you can't keep drinking *and* complain about getting fat. Alcohol makes you bloated, period. It's one of the most calorific substances on the planet. Having said that, if you switch to Mai Tais, you definitely won't be able to drink as many of them as you could beers. When I was on the booze, beers didn't even count, I could knock 'em back so easily. Some people might say, 'Try pot,' but then you'll get the munchies, which is just as bad. My advice would be to cut down on the beer. Or stop drinking altogether.

Dear Dr Ozzy:
I love having a full-strength Marlboro before breakfast, but I've noticed that the first couple of drags make me

want to run to the bathroom and evacuate. Is this
normal?
David, Cardiff

If you're a smoker, why the fuck are you wasting time worrying about your bowels? What about your *lungs*? Having
said that, though, nicotine is a stimulant, so that world-
falling-out-of-your-arse feeling is normal. Why not give up
smoking and have a glass of orange juice instead? You
know, over the years, I've taken every drug known to man,
and I swear nicotine is the worst. Take it from the Prince
of Darkness: cigarettes are evil.

Dear Dr Ozzy:
I noticed that you worked with a personal trainer during
The Osbournes. Did you find it helpful?
James, Scarborough, Maine

Using a trainer helped me keep to a routine, which is very
helpful, 'cos I'm an all-or-nothing kind of guy: I'll kill
myself on the treadmill one month, then spend the next
with my head in the fridge. But after a while I got pissed
off with a guy standing there in my own house, shouting,
'Do another five reps.' I almost chinned the bastard a
couple of times.

Dear Dr Ozzy:
I've recently decided to slow down my hedonistic
lifestyle and try being healthy, so now it's all low-fat
food and exercise. But when I wake up in the morning, I
feel worse than I did before. How long will this last, or
should I just return to my old ways?
Alex, Milton Keynes

Rome wasn't built in a day. Some people go over the top when they try to get healthy: one minute they're living a life of beer, cheeseburgers and daytime telly; the next they've cut out meat, alcohol, coffee and sugar, and they're trying to run a marathon. *Of course* you're gonna feel like shit if you do that. Take it easy. One thing at a time. And if you're doing exercise, for God's sake make sure you stretch before and afterwards.

> **Dear Dr Ozzy:**
> **What's the healthiest (and most effective) way to administer a jolt of caffeine first thing in the morning: a shot of espresso or a full-sized mug of filter coffee?**
> **Anonymous, Pittsburgh**

I don't know about the *healthiest*, but I can tell you the *best* way — by a mile. First of all, brew yourself a normal pot of filter coffee. Then tip the coffee back into the filter and brew it again over the old grounds. At the same time, make yourself an espresso. Next step: pour yourself a cup of the double-strength filter coffee. Then add the shot of espresso. I call it a 'red eye': one sip and you'll be as awake as you've even been in your life, trust me. That ain't the strongest coffee I've ever had, mind you. My old mate Frank Zappa used to make a brew that tasted like leaded petrol. And Turkish coffee is even worse. I downed a soup bowl of that stuff when I was in Crete once, and then spent the next three weeks jogging around the island, trying to get it to wear off.

> **Dear Dr Ozzy:**
> **Why do people say it's bad to eat chocolate before public speaking (or singing, for that matter)?**
> **Jim, Kelso**

Well, for a start, chocolate thickens your saliva, which ain't good news if you've gotta recite Shakespeare or get through 'Iron Man'. For me, chocolate also causes heartburn, which sends acid shooting up my oesophagus, literally burning my throat – and that's my worst fear when I'm on the road, 'cos it affects thousands of people when a show is cancelled. Having said that, you're not supposed to drink tea, either, but I still do before every gig. It might not be very rock 'n'roll, but it's like a magic potion to me.

> **Dear Dr Ozzy:**
> I know you work out a lot and have changed your lifestyle dramatically, but is it more difficult to maintain your exercise schedule and health regimen when you are touring? What do you recommend for people like me who pretty much live on the road?
> John, Santa Barbara

To be honest, I don't need to go to the gym when I'm on the road. During a two-hour show, I'll burn about two thousand calories and use muscles I don't even know I have until the next day, when I feel like I've been thrown off the Empire State Building. But I've got one piece of advice for anyone who works away from home in a sedentary job: *go for a walk*. It's one of the best forms of exercise there is, and it costs nothing. The only reason I don't go for walks myself is because my arse has got a mind of its own, and if I'm out of range of a toilet, I freak out. That shouldn't stop anybody else, though.

> **Dear Dr Ozzy:**
> I'm pretty much living on five-hour energy drinks. Is this stuff gonna hurt me in the long run?
> Eric, Colorado

Well, it's not exactly food, is it? You're basically just shoot-ing up caffeine. And if there's one golden rule I've learned over the years, it's this: *what goes up must come down.* I remember necking a few energy drinks before going on stage once: I felt like the king of the universe for about one-and-a-half songs, but by the third number I was ready to fucking hang myself. So, if I were you, I'd try to get your energy from something that's not gonna make you drop like the *Hindenburg* when the rush wears off.

Dear Dr Ozzy:
I'm in my mid-fifties and a stonking twenty-five stones.
I'm addicted to food, often eating enough for three or
four people. I'm out of breath, have no interest in sex,
and can hardly even stand up. I'm using food like you
used drugs – I'm killing myself. Any advice? Money is
no object.
John, London

Number one, find a good dietician. Number two, start exer-cising (as long as your doc gives you the okay). But whatever you do, *don't* go mental. For example: start at the lowest set-ting on the treadmill, then work your way up *slowly*. The mistake I made was thinking: Well, if I turn this thing up to warp factor ten, I'll burn more calories. But I wasn't fit enough, my legs couldn't keep up, and I almost catapulted myself backwards through a plate-glass window. Another thing is to find an activity you enjoy, 'cos if you don't love it, you ain't gonna stick at it. But you've got to do more than take up darts or table football. You've gotta break a sweat. I'm twelve-and-a-half stones at the moment, but I could easily be twenty-five myself if I didn't burn off all the crap I eat with a bit of exercise. Fortunately, I've now become addicted to the blast of endorphins you get on a cross-trainer, in exactly the same way I used to be addicted to Special Brew. I've also got a massive telly in my gym at home, so while I'm getting rid of my extra chins I can watch Second World War documentaries on the History Channel. That's my idea of paradise – a bit of cardio and some animated battle maps.

> **Dear Dr Ozzy:**
> I recently went to Cuba, picked up a nasty bug, and was hospitalised with dehydration. The doctors shoved a steel lozenge thing down my throat to take a biopsy from my stomach, but it didn't find the cause of the problem. Three months later, I'm still passing liquid. Please help.
> Simon, Doncaster

Three months? If I was passing liquid for three *hours* I'd be straight down the gastroenterologist's, begging him to make it stop. Chances are it was some dodgy lettuce that did it. Let me tell you something: lettuce is fucking deadly if you eat it in the wrong country. I mean, yeah, you think it's all nice and posh and healthy and whatever, but if you order a salad in some parts of Mexico or South America, you might as well order a plate of raw human shit, 'cos that's what's in the water they've washed it in. I've suffered the same fate on more than a few occasions: you cross the border into Mexico and within a few hours you're laid up in hospital on a drip. But three months is no joke: it could even be more serious than you think, so get it checked out again.

> **Dear Dr Ozzy:**
> I want to reduce the calories I eat, but how on earth do you go about counting them? I know that everything you

buy in the supermarket has those little stickers on it
now, but does anyone seriously measure out every
single portion? And what about food you eat in
restaurants, or that other people cook for you? How can
you keep track of it all without dedicating your entire
life to it?
Brian, Castle Bromwich

It's a total waste of time, counting calories. For example, I
looked at a packet of cereal the other day, and it said on the
side, 'One bowl – 230 calories'. But how big's the bowl? For
all I know, it could be the size of an ashtray or a swimming
pool. A better strategy is just to cut down your portions.
Using smaller plates is a good idea. Seriously. Here in
America, they give you enough food in one sandwich to
feed the North Korean Army for a month. It's only when
you put it on a normal-sized plate that you realise what a pig
you're being. Exercise also makes a really big difference, even
if it's just a twenty-minute walk every day. Do both of those
things, and you'll never have to count calories again.

Dear Dr Ozzy:
What's the best way to treat a burned mouth? I love
food, so there's nothing worse than getting
overenthusiastic about a piping-hot meal and
destroying my taste buds for a week.
Sam, Warwick

I've done that with a hot chip before now, and it's horrible.
It's even worse when you get it stuck halfway down your
windpipe – then everything you eat for the next month
tastes like sulphuric fucking acid. You've gotta *slow down*,
man. In England, we eat food like it could jump up and do

the hundred-yard dash at any second. Alternatively, you could eat all your meals at a restaurant with lazy waiters, so the food's always lukewarm.

> **Dear Dr Ozzy:**
> **Why are people so worried about the mercury in tuna? I read the other day that Abraham Lincoln used to take mercury-laced pills to treat his constipation, and he was in good enough health to lead America (until he was shot, of course).**
> **Percy, Cardiff**

I'd only be worried about the mercury in tuna if I ate a whole one. Otherwise, I can't see how a bit of sushi every now and then is a problem. Having said that, a friend of my daughter recently got mercury poisoning, and it was heavy duty, man: she had memory loss, slurred speech, crazy mood swings, loss of coordination. Basically, she ended up feeling how I did during most of the 1980s. As for good old Abe Lincoln, it's never a good idea to say something like, 'So-and-so used to put leeches on his eyeballs, so it must be okay.' I mean, they used to add heroin to cough mixture. If they still did that today, I'd be off sick with a cold 365 days a year.

> **Dear Dr Ozzy:**
> **People keep banging on about how great yoga is – especially when it comes to stress – but I can't stand the thought of all that chanting and hippy-dippy bullshit. Have you ever tried it?**
> **Sam, Beaconsfield**

You've got totally the wrong idea. Doing yoga ain't like being a Buddhist monk. Or at least it doesn't have to be.

It's basically just stretching exercises – and you'd be amazed at the results you can get. I used to have this make-up artist, and she left to have a baby. I saw her a year later, after she'd done a lot of yoga, and she looked amazing, all slim and tight and healthy. You'd never have believed she'd pushed one out just a few months earlier. Personally, I've just started a Pilates course for the same reason. I'm not out of shape, but I want to avoid getting a big old gut on me. My only fear with these stretching-based things is that I won't have the patience. Generally speaking, if I haven't worked up a sweat in the first three seconds, I'm off. So we'll see if I can stick at it. In the meantime, why don't you take a leaf out of my book, and at least *try* it.

DR OZZY'S INSANE-BUT-TRUE-STORIES

When Exercise is Bad For You

➕ Next time you're in the gym, watch out for blokes with exploding balls – exercise balls, that is. One guy in Florida sued after the one he was leaning on (while holding two dumb-bells) went pop, sending him crashing to the floor. He needed five surgeries, allegedly.

➕ No one knew you could get high from endorphins until a guy called Jim Fixx came along in the 1970s. He was basically a fat bloke who smoked two packets of fags a day until he started jogging. He lost the flab, quit tobacco, and turned himself into the world's first fitness guru. Trouble was, he dropped dead at fifty-two ... while on a run.

■ Scientists reckon the chance of ending up like Fixx – croaking it while exercising – is about 1 in 18,000.* People who work out the most have a higher risk than those who do the least. Being fat ain't much of an alternative, though: obesity is a much more common preventable cause of death.

■ During the 1956 FA Cup Final, Man City's goalie, Bert Trautmann, managed to break his neck after diving for the ball one too many times. There were still seventeen minutes to go, though, so the crazy fucker just kept on playing – and even made a few more heroic saves that helped his team take home the cup. The guy didn't even bother getting an X-ray until three days later, when he finally realised his head was about to fall off. He made a full recovery and, now in his late eighties, he's still going strong.

Dear Dr Ozzy:
I keep hearing that humans need to drink eight glasses of water a day. Surely this is bullshit?
Billy, Leicester

I tried drinking eight glasses of water a day for a while, and my bladder felt like a red-hot fucking cannon ball. I need to pee a lot as it is, so I'd have to live in the bog if I was knocking back two litres of water each day. My advice is this: if you eat a lot of fruit and vegetables, you'll get some water from your food. On the top of that, drink as much

---

* According to the *New England Journal of Medicine*.

as you need to stop being thirsty. Obviously, if you sweat during exercise, you'll be thirstier, and you'll need to drink a bit more. That's what animals do to survive in the wild, and we ain't any different.

> Dear Dr Ozzy:
> I've become addicted to counting calories. I have a sensor in my shoes that sends a 'calorie burn readout' to my iPhone. I input everything I eat into a calorie counting website. And I try to estimate how many calories I'm burning up doing everything else (including typing this). I'm losing weight, but going insane. Advice?
> William, Berkshire

I remember seeing an interview with Bob Dylan after he wrote his memoirs, and he said, 'While you're writing, you ain't living.' The same goes for counting calories – which I've tried to do on many occasions. The bottom line is, every minute you spend jotting down every last cornflake or baked bean you ate during the day is a minute you could have spent with your family or friends. Either that or you could use the time to learn something, like a new language. Okay, you'd still be fat, but at least you'd be fat and could order a double cheeseburger in Slovakian.

> Dear Dr Ozzy:
> I haven't been able to 'go' for ten days, and I'm starting to get really worried. Nothing seems able to unclog me.
> Barry, Aberdeen

I'd usually recommend a strong cup of coffee, but it sounds more like you need a stick of dynamite. Prunes can also be effective, if you can stand the taste. Personally, if I'm suffering from a spot of constipation, I'll ask the missus for some of her 'special tummy pills'. All women seem to have a stash of these things somewhere – not that you'd know what they do from the packaging. The box doesn't have a picture of a giant steaming turd on the front, put it that way. Sharon's pills come in a pink box with flowers on it. Be careful, though: I once took a handful of 'em, thinking they'd never work – nothing else had – but boy, was I wrong. Two minutes later, I was unloading about ten Christmas dinners out of my rear end. And it continued that way for days, to the point where I couldn't even work out where all the stuff was coming from. It was like the laws of physics didn't apply. So I suggest getting hold of the same stuff. *But go easy with it.*

Dear Dr Ozzy:
I love lattes, but just one medium cup gives me a headache and makes my heart race. Is this normal?
Anne, Tyneside

I learned the answer to this question when I got my DNA analysed on a computer in 2010: we all metabolise caffeine at different speeds, based on the way our genes work. Personally, I feel like my head is about to blast off to Mars after one sip of espresso, and now I know why: my body just can't process it. It sounds like you're built the same way. Unfortunately, there's only one thing you can do: switch to another drink. Trying to beat your own genes is a game you're only ever gonna lose.

Dear Dr Ozzy:
How much vitamin C is healthy? I'm taking 4000mg a day in the hope of avoiding a cold.
Meredith, Surrey

I'm pretty sure your body can store only so much vitamin C: the rest just passes straight through you. So even if you take five million milligrams, it won't do you much good. The sad fact is, if you're gonna get the flu . . . you're gonna get the flu.

> **Dear Dr Ozzy:**
> Every time I drink milk I get the most horrific eggy flatulence you've ever had the misfortune to smell. I can clear out entire restaurants with it. Does this mean I'm 'lactose intolerant', or is that just some bollocks that Hollywood types have invented?
> Glen, London

It ain't bullshit. I've got a friend who literally turns green when she drinks milk. Try switching to soy milk for week, then wait until a good old rumbler comes down the pipe, and let it loose in a confined area. If everyone's still conscious after five minutes, problem solved.

> **Dear Dr Ozzy:**
> During important meetings, my stomach growls loud enough for everyone in the room to hear. It happens even after I've eaten a good breakfast. Please help – it's terribly awkward.
> Terry, Belfast

Nerves. I guarantee it. It might even be a symptom of IBS (irritable bowel syndrome). At least you're not breaking wind, though: that's *really* embarrassing. Trust me. Especially when it sends a stale breeze through the room. That's the thing about the human brain: when it's stressed out, it'll find all kinds of ways to mess with you – from making you feel like you need to pee all the time to bringing you out in a rash. Which is doubly horrible, 'cos those things just make the original problem worse. The good news is that there are all kinds of potions you can take to help you calm down, including a special kind of beta blocker that they use for stage fright. Ask your GP about it.

> Dear Dr Ozzy:
> I've joined a cycling club to get fit, and a lot of my fellow members – all men – have told me that I should shave my legs to become 'more aerodynamic'. Isn't that a bit weird? I mean, how much more aerodynamic can you possibly become by removing a few leg hairs?
> Jim, Exeter

Unless they start asking you to wear ladies' knickers, I wouldn't worry about it. Also, from what I understand, the shaving has nothing to do with aerodynamics – it just makes it easier to treat a leg injury if you fall off, which happens a lot if you compete in heavy-duty road races.

> Dear Dr Ozzy:
> Whenever I eat, or have a 'number two', my nose runs continually. I'm not joking – it's driving me bananas. What can I do about this (other than buying shares in Kleenex)?
> Jacky (no address given)
> PS: I'm not allergic to anything as far as I know.

All kinds of crazy things can make your nose run, because of the way your ears, nose and throat are all linked together. I get bunged up all the time 'cos of everything from dust mites to dodgy smells, so you might want to investigate allergies a bit more. See your doc and ask what he thinks about you trying antihistamines. Washing out your sinuses regularly with saline spray might help, too. Be careful, though – if you do it wrong, it feels like you're being fucking waterboarded. You could also be reacting to the temperature of the food you're eating, or how spicy it is. For instance, if I ate a lamb vindaloo every day, I know my nose would run. As for the 'number twos' – that's pretty far out, man. Maybe the sensation of pushing is triggering the same thing as the food? When you see your GP, ask if he can send you to an ear, nose and throat guy for a consultation.

> Dear Dr Ozzy:
> Every so often, I get these nasty little bumps on my tongue which ruin my sense of taste. Please help.
> Saeed, Leeds

By the sound of your question, this has happened to you a number times, and the bumps have come and gone without making your tongue fall out or your head explode. So why are you worrying? Having said that, if it were me and something weird puffed up somewhere, I'd be straight down the doc's to get it checked out. Given that you've gone to the trouble of writing in, it's obviously bothering you too, so you should do the same.

> Dear Dr Ozzy:
> Is it true that eating a big meal late at night makes you fatter than if you ate the same meal for lunch?
> Dolly, Hereford

It depends. I mean, if you're a competitive eater who can shove ninety-eight cream pies down her throat in four minutes, then I doubt you'd put on less weight if you ate 'em for breakfast instead of dinner. On the other hand, if you have a normal diet, it seems logical that it's better to eat as early as you can – not only so your body has a chance to metabolise the food, but to prevent acid reflux syndrome. The trouble is, if I don't have a good meal at night, I can't sleep, especially after a two-hour gig. So I'll end up having a salad, then, five minutes later, ordering a pizza. That's why I've gotta watch myself on the road – I wanna be the Prince of Darkness, not the Prince of Fatness.

> **Dear Dr Ozzy:**
> My husband wants to take me to a sushi restaurant for the first time. Is there anything I should avoid for health reasons, or is all the stuff I've heard about the dangers of raw fish overblown?
> Zara, Durham

The thing to remember about sushi – Western-style sushi, anyway – is that it ain't like the smelly old haddock you used to get from the fishmonger when you were little. From what I understand, sushi-grade fish is bled, gutted and packed in ice very, very quickly. And it is usually frozen long enough to kill any parasites that might cause you problems. Having said that, I'd still avoid fugu if it's on the menu (see page 20).

> **Dear Dr Ozzy:**
> I need to lose weight – fast – for a wedding. Are diet pills a good idea?
> Ben, Stevenage

It's up to you – as long as you bear in mind that some of those pills come with pretty heavy side-effects, like 'gas with oily spotting'. You don't want to break wind during the best man's speech and feel like the *Deepwater Horizon* just sprang a leak in your underwear.

> Dear Dr Ozzy:
> I've just read about an eighty-two-year-old man in India – his name is Prahlad Jani – who claims not to have eaten a single thing since 1942. (He hasn't drunk anything either, allegedly.) He says he draws nourishment from meditation. Could this be possible, given that the longest-ever hunger strike went on for just seventy-four days?
> Derek, Peebles

I don't know, but I'm gonna get my assistant on the phone ASAP and send this guy a curry – he must be *starving*. Actually, the whole thing seems pretty fishy to me. I mean, there's no way I could meditate – or go without a hot dinner – for that long. I'm ready to throw a brick at someone after sitting cross-legged for sixty-nine seconds, never mind sixty-nine years.

Chapter Notes:
Fitness Methods
(Cut Out and Keep)

	Running	Swimming	Cycling	Weight-lifting	Yoga
Handy tip	Start your workout close to something that might kill you – you'll run faster	Some holiday resorts have bars in their pools	If you like cross-dressing, this is the best excuse you'll ever get for shaving your legs	You can get paid to do this ... by becoming a professional bag carrier	Find the best-looking woman in the class and stand behind her – it'll cheer you up no end
Dangers & annoyances	The thing that might kill you ... might actually kill you. Also beware of: ball chafing, heart attacks	Some pools with bars have yellow fucking water. Also beware of: sharks, rip-tides, overly tight trunks	Saying 'But darling, it's for aero-dynamic reasons' ain't gonna fly if you're also wearing fishnets and a bra	Looking like a weight-lifter	Bulges can be spotted easily through Lycra
Pay-off	Feeling healthy 'cos you're wearing a tracksuit	When you get tired, you can always float	Putting on silk stockings without them ripping	Looking like a weight-lifter	Being able to jump off a drum riser while doing the splits – and not waking up in hospital

Dr Ozzy's Trivia Quiz:
Health Nut

*Find the answers – and add up
your score – on page 278*

1. **If you ate *one* tablespoon each of these foods, which would slam you with the most calories?**

a) Goose fat
b) Ghee (clarified butter, used in curries)
c) Unsalted butter

2. **Farting less often is easy if you ...**

a) Swallow less air
b) Drink more water
c) Cut down on beans, sugar-free chewing gum ... and pears

3. **Speaking of unwanted trouser explosions ... how many times does the average person let rip every day?**

a) 14 times (1–4 pints of gas)
b) Twice (half a pint of gas)
c) 27 times (8–12 pints of gas)

4. What causes 'heavy leg syndrome'?

a) Involvement with the Mafia

b) Exercising too much

c) Not enough blood circulation

5. How old was the fitness guru/muscleman Jack LaLanne when he died?

a) 41

b) 96

c) 73

3

Pruning

Cleanliness is Next to Ozzyness

When I was growing up in Aston, my idea of personal grooming was a hot bath every other year. It's not like there was a lot of pressure to be smooth-skinned and beautiful in those days. As a bloke, you were hairy and smelly, full stop, end of story. And as a bloke who was also a rock 'n'roll singer, you were basically a one-man walking fucking sewer. I went on tour in Scandinavia once – in the depths of winter – with only one change of underpants. And no toothpaste. By the time I got back on the ferry to Harwich, my breath was so bad, every time I opened my mouth to say something, flowers wilted and birds fell out of the sky.

I'm a new man now.

The first time I really experienced modern beauty treatments was when I met Sharon. I woke up one day and she had me in a headlock with a pair of tweezers in her hand. I remember screaming, 'What the fuck are you DOING?!'

She just tightened her grip and said, 'I'm giving you a long-overdue pruning, Ozzy, that's what I'm fucking doing.'

That's what Sharon calls it: 'pruning'. And she does it to me at every available opportunity. If she sees so much as a single nose hair – she calls 'em 'Hitlers' 'cos they look like the Führer's moustache – she'll go after it like a lioness going after her prey. After a while, I gave up trying to escape, 'cos putting up a fight wasn't worth the pain. By holding out, I was making only one person miserable: *me*. Besides, I didn't exactly want to go around looking like three different families of crows had set up a nest in my conk.

It's reached the point these days where I actually enjoy a good pruning – especially if it involves a long massage before a gig. I might be the Prince of Darkness, but I've had more pedicures than I've had hot dinners. I don't take it too far, though. I've never had my balls waxed. My anus has never been bleached. And I ain't into all that 'caviar facial' bollocks.

To me, looking good is about working with what you've got, and taking care of the simple things. Then again, if something *really* bothers you, I ain't got any bones about saying, 'Get it fixed.' Going under the knife once in a while doesn't mean you automatically end up like Michael Jackson or that crazy Cat Woman in New York. You've just gotta make sure you save up enough dough to pay for a top-notch doctor. And you've gotta know when enough's enough. In the meantime, you'll be amazed what you can achieve with a bit of regular maintenance, which is what this chapter's all about.

Dear Dr Ozzy:
I'm a twenty-four-year-old single man with a big date coming up, and I want to make sure I look good in the

buff – y'know, just in case. With that in mind, should I
trim my armpit hair?
Simon, Bethnal Green

How long can your armpit hair possibly be, man? I mean,
I could understand if you were worried about the hair on
your head, or the smell of your cologne, or what clothes to
wear – but unless you're planning to get this poor woman in
a nude headlock over dinner, how the fuck do your armpits
come into the equation? Since you asked, though, let me
give you some man-to-man advice: I shaved my armpits
once, for a joke, and it hurt like you wouldn't believe for
a whole month. Worse than that, they broke out in an 'or-
rible pimply rash. So, if I were you, I'd leave your armpits
well alone and concentrate on something else, like your
conversation skills.

Dear Dr Ozzy:
I can't resist the temptation to squeeze my blackheads
and spots, even though I know I'm not supposed to. Is
this bad? Does anyone seriously just wait until they pop
by themselves?
Chris, Kent

None of my spots ever goes unsqueezed … because of
Sharon: if she sees one, she'll be at it with a hammer and
chisel in a heartbeat. You're right, though: you're not supposed to start hacking away at your forehead. If you do,
you'll leave behind a scar, give yourself an infection, or
force that white gunky stuff in the wrong direction, making
you look like the Elephant Man. If you've got a bit of
dough in the bank, go and see a good facialist and they'll
do the squeezing for you. Pressing a hot towel to your face

and then massaging the pores can also help. Whatever you do, make sure you wash your hands thoroughly first.

> **Dear Dr Ozzy:**
> **My ears stick out at right angles. I wouldn't mind if they did something more useful – like picking up Sky Sports – but they just make me look like an idiot. What should I do?**
> **Neil, Glasgow**

No one wants to walk around the place looking like the Ryder Cup. But I think you're being a bit hard on your poor old lugs – the job of hearing is pretty important (take it from someone who's half deaf). And Prince Charles does all right with his ears, which he could rent out at the weekend as parasails. But my advice is always the same with these things: if it bothers you, *do something about it*. Yes, the operation might be expensive, but buying an iPad or a new telly is also expensive, and no one ever seems to have a problem saving up dough for something like that. If your ears are making you miserable, it might be the best investment you ever make.

> **Dear Dr Ozzy:**
> **I'm in my mid-thirties and, sadly, losing my hair. Should I resign myself to my fate or fight it by any means necessary? How do you maintain your manly flowing locks?**
> **Leo, Maryland**

I've always been blessed with good hair. I don't wear a rug. I don't wear extensions. And I don't use spray paint to touch up bald spots. The only thing I do to my hair is dye it. In fact, I've always promised myself that if I ever start getting threadbare on top, I'll shave it all off rather than getting an Irish (Irish jig = wig) or spending half the day trying to arrange my last three stands into a greasy comb-over. I mean, whenever I see those guys with crazy rugs, or the ones who wear cowboy hats all the time, I just wanna say, 'Fuck off, we all know you ain't got any hair.' And while it's possible to buy some very good wigs these days – if you've got the time, the dough, and the patience – most of 'em are ludicrous. One time in a bar in New York, I next to a bloke with the worst wig I'd seen in my life. It looked like a cat had died on his head. I mean, buying a wig is one thing, but why would you go for a *ginger* one? In the end, I reached up, pulled it off, and used it to mop up my spilled beer. The guy went fucking mental. But if it taught him to be bald and proud, I did him a favour.

DR OZZY'S AMAZING MEDICAL MISCELLANY

Beauty Secrets Through the Ages

- If you've got bad skin, try using a three-inch-deep layer of white powder foundation to cover it. Then add some smudged eye-liner and fake blood. It won't get you laid, but it'll get you out of babysitting duties for the rest of your life.

- They say that putting a cold tea bag on a bruise will make it vanish faster. If a doctor ever asks if you're up for a bit of 'tea-bagging', though, it's best to say 'no'. He might mean something else.

- If a bird craps on your head while you're standing under a tree, wave and say thanks. In Japan, that's considered a hundred-quid-a-go facial treatment. (The stuff they use is a powder made from nightingale shit.)

- In the Philippines, mothers have been known to cut their baby's eyelashes 'cos they think it makes them grow back longer and darker when they're older. Personally, I wouldn't trust anyone to hold a pair of sharp scissors anywhere near a baby's eyeballs. The kid ain't gonna thank you for his long eyelashes if he needs a white fucking stick to cross the road.

- If you think rinsing out your mouth with Listerine tastes bad, you should have been around in ancient Roman times, when good dental hygiene involved gargling with piss (as long as it came from a Portuguese person). Mind you, I've had a few pints of beer in America that probably tasted worse.

Dear Dr Ozzy:
I'm thinking of getting some cosmetic surgery done, but I feel very self-conscious about anyone seeing me with bandages over my face during the recovery period. I'm also concerned about the stares I'm going to get when I show up in the office with a completely different face. What's the best way to handle all this?
Sarah, Keswick

What exactly are you planning to do when your face is all bandaged up – go clubbing for a week in Ibiza? You're gonna have to stay indoors and rest after the operation, so you won't need to see anyone unless you want to. Over in California, they put you up in a special hotel where there's a whole floor for recovering patients. If it's a two-bob job, obviously you ain't gonna get that kind of service, but in that case I'd recommend that you wait until you can afford a better surgeon. As for the last part of your question: I don't understand why you're altering your appearance in the first place if you're worried about people *noticing* the changes. It sounds like you haven't thought this through. If I were you, I'd put everything on hold until you've had a long talk with a therapist and sorted out everything in your head.

> **Dear Dr Ozzy:**
> I'm a man of very limited stature (five feet). Should I buy platform shoes or will that make me look sillier?
> **Gary, Belfast**

Depends on the shoes. I ain't short, but I used to wear these silver, glittery platform soles in the 1970s, and I thought they looked the dog's bollocks. Mind you, I was doing a lot of acid at the time. My advice to you is not to worry so much about what other people think. If you don't mind being short, be short. And if you want to look like you're in Abba, go for the platforms.

> **Dear Dr Ozzy:**
> How can I get my skin to be as flawless as yours?
> **Nora, Dublin**

All I do is use a good natural cream – nothing fancy, not the two-grand-a-bottle bullshit – every morning and every night. What you've got to remember is that your face is out in the elements all the time, which means it has to deal with sun, dust, grime and all other kinds of other crap. Also, as skin ages, it gets drier, so you need to blast it with as much moisture as possible. Personally, I don't bother with facials, unless Sharon has someone over to the house and ropes me into it. She's got skin creams up the fucking yin-yang – which I suppose is all right if you're a woman. But speaking as the owner of a pair of testicles, I like to keep my daily grooming time to the bare minimum.

> **Dear Dr Ozzy:**
> I was looking at some holiday pictures recently and realised – with horror – that I have a quadruple chin. I look like a cross between my grandma and a concertina. Help!
> John, Hastings

I used to have more chins than a Chinese phone book. It's a genetic thing with my family – we all have this balloon of fat under our jaws. When I complained to my GP about it, he told me to grow a beard, but I didn't want to do that. So, in the end, I fixed it with liposuction. They stick a needle into the blubber, suck it out, and send you away with a bandage around your face, like you've just had the worst dentist's appointment of your life. Luckily, I didn't notice the pain, 'cos I was still blasted all the time in those days. It's like I always say, if something bothers you every time you look in the mirror, and if the technology exists to sort it out, and if you've got the dough, then do it. It certainly changed my life.

Dear Dr Ozzy:
Plucking my eyebrows makes me sneeze! Why do you
think this is, and how can I stop it happening?
Louise, Essex

I have exactly the same problem. Putting on eye make-up
before a gig always sends the snot flying in all directions –
my green room is *literally* a green room. I think it's due to
your sinuses, which go all the way up your face to your
eyebrow area. So when you pluck your eyebrows, you're
basically tickling your sinuses. The bad news is that the only
way to stop it happening is to stop plucking. So you either
have to put up with the occasional sneezing fit, or get ready
to start looking like a walking hedgerow.

Dear Dr Ozzy:
I was born with a pale complexion but would love to get
a suntan – people with brown skin look so much
healthier. What's the best way to do this without
resorting to tin foil?
Vicky, Sunderland

Whatever you do, *don't* go to an old-fashioned tanning
salon. I went to one of those joints once, turned the
machine straight up to level ten-and-a-half, and passed out
on the bed. I woke up a few hours later looking like I'd
been hit by an atomic bomb. I was furious with myself for
months 'cos I could hardly walk – never mind smile, or
bend over, or do anything that involved creasing even the
tiniest part of my skin. I might as well have paid someone
to throw me in a bath of acid – it probably would have been
less painful. It ages you by decades, too. A few doses of the
hard stuff and you'll end up with a face like an eighteenth-

century football. I urge you to avoid anything to do with UV rays – they're far too dangerous for my liking – and get one of those quickie spray-on jobs instead. It won't last long, and you might smell a bit funny the day after, but it won't give you third-degree burns or cancer.

> **Dear Dr Ozzy:**
> What's the best way to get rid of warts?
> Tim, Dartmouth

Antifreeze and fire. I don't recommend it, though.

> **Dear Dr Ozzy:**
> I'm in my mid-forties and am stunned to find that my hair is turning white (not the hair on my head). I thought I could use dye, but some hairs are still black and I don't want to look like a tabby. It's getting me down and is starting to affect my love life, which I was hoping to reignite with the help of the local plastic surgeon before it's too late. Help!
> Katy, Buckinghamshire

Personally, I've never had a bikini wax, and I don't know why any bloke in his right mind would ever let another bloke anywhere near his nearest and dearest. For women, though, it's a lot more common – and, in your case, it sounds like the lawnmower treatment might not be a bad idea. Just don't get carried away. Over in LA, some women get this thing called 'revirgination' (where they repair the hymen), while gay blokes are bleaching parts of their bodies that should never even see the light of day. I wouldn't recommend any of that. But a bit of hot wax might do the trick for you.

Dear Dr Ozzy:
I recently lost a lot of weight and now I have horrendous
stretch marks. How can I get rid of them?
Michael, Kent

That's the problem with losing weight as you get older: the
dreaded stretch marks. Either that or all the elasticity in
your skin disappears, so you end up with a big, floppy bag
of skin hanging over your arse. I've got to ask you a question, though: *where* are these stretch marks? If they're under
your clothes, why bother? Who cares? Otherwise, have a
look on the Internet for all the oils and potions you can put
on your skin, or ask your doc about laser treatment. Getting
yourself zapped can be very pricey, but I'm told it can also
be very effective.

Dear Dr Ozzy:
I'm desperate to get some tattoos, but I'm broke, and
my parents won't help me out because they don't
approve. Can I do them myself with a needle and some
ink, like you did?
Jason, Cardiff

Yes, you can do it yourself, but I strongly advise you not to.
All kinds of things can go wrong if you start stabbing yourself with a rusty fork. I got my first tattoo while I was doing
time for burglary in Winson Green Prison, Birmingham:
anything to make the days go by quicker. One of the guys
drew a picture of The Saint on my arm with a ballpoint
pen – I'd been a fan of the show since it started in 1962 –
then used a sewing pin he'd nicked from the workroom and
some melted grate polish (the stuff they used to clean fire-
places) to poke the tattoo over the top. After that, I was

hooked. I once spent a whole afternoon in Sutton Park, a posh part of town, spelling out 'O-Z-Z-Y' across my knuckles. Then I put a smiley face on each of my knees to cheer myself up when I was sitting on the bog one morning. My old man wasn't very fucking impressed, mind you. He took one look at me, shook his head, and went, 'Son, you're an *idiot.*'

Dr Ozzy's Trivia Quiz:
Being Beautiful

*Find the answers – and add up
your score – on page 279*

1. **What crazy beauty secret did Cleopatra use to look good?**

a) Smearing crocodile shit on her face
b) Putting asses' milk up her ass
c) Banning mirrors in her house

2. **Which of these unlikely ingredients have been found in baldness cures throughout history?**

a) Burnt mice
b) Ground horses' teeth
c) 'Bear grease', whatever the fuck that is

3. **If you sit for a long time behind a car window on a sunny day, what's most likely to happen?**

a) You'll tan faster than the cast of *The Only Way is Essex*
b) You won't get tanned, but you'll burn like Guy Fawkes on 5 November
c) You won't tan or burn ... but people will start mistaking you for Yoda

4. **Who spent $24,000 (more or less) on a single haircut in 2009?**

a) Tony Blair
b) Michael Jackson
c) The Sultan of Brunei

5. **What do the Czechs bathe in before and/or after drinking beer?**

a) More beer
b) Horse sweat
c) Sausage fat

4

Family – The Other F-Word

You Love 'Em to Death, but They Drive You Fucking Mental

Last Christmas, my wife had one of her brilliant ideas. 'Ozzy,' she said one morning. 'Let's go to England, get all the kids together, and have a traditional family Christmas in our house in the English Countryside. It'll be lovely. What do you think?'

'Are you *sure*?' I said. 'The kids are grown up now. Maybe they'll want to do their own thing.'

'Oh, Ozzy,' she said. '*Of course* they'll want to be with their mum and dad. Besides, it's the house where they all grew up.'

I wasn't convinced. 'Look, Sharon,' I said. 'Are you *absolutely* sure you know what you're doing?'

'Of course!' she replied.

Needless to say, it was a fucking disaster. Peace on earth? It would have been more peaceful if we'd gone to Tripoli. Could the kids get along with each other for more than five seconds? *Not on your life*. If it wasn't one, it was the other. All I could hear were slammed doors, house-plants being thrown across the room, and people screaming at each other. It was so bad at one point, I almost fell off the wagon and had a beer. Finally, on Christmas Day, I got up, went downstairs and said to everyone, 'Look: all I want for Christmas is for you to get on, even if you have to fake it – *just for one fucking day!*'

Everyone nodded, hung their heads, and agreed to calm down. It lasted three hours. Then they were back at it again, worse than before. It broke my heart, to be honest – and it broke Sharon's, too. I was just so disappointed, y'know? But you can only do so much with your kids; then you've just got to let 'em get on with it. The thing is, everyone wants the perfect family . . . but it doesn't exist.

We all dream of our cosy little domestic get-togethers, where everyone says how much they love each other, everyone remembers the good times, and no one gets angry or jealous or has any issues. But as Dr Ozzy, I've come to realise that all families are made up of human beings, and human beings are by their very nature messy and emotional and full of all kinds of fears and insecurities. If that sounds familiar to you, I recommend you read on, 'cos this chapter takes you through just about every issue you're ever likely to face with your own flesh and blood, from the womb to the nursing home.

BASIC PARENTING

Dear Dr Ozzy:
My husband and I are trying to have a second baby, and we'd love it to be a girl. Is there anything we can do in

the bedroom department to skew the odds in our favour?
Pamela, London

I've heard lots of wacky theories about 'gender swaying' over the years: do it standing on your head for a boy; keep your left sock on for a girl; drink lemon juice for a boy; cranberry juice for a girl . . . etc., etc. It's all bollocks, if you ask me, and the bottom line is, even if you want a girl and you get a boy, you ain't gonna love him any less. And there's something to be said for the surprise. When Sharon and I had our son, Jack, we had no idea what sex he was, 'cos he was lying in a funny position when they did the sonogram. In fact, we were convinced he was gonna be a girl, 'cos we had two daughters already, so when he popped out with a full set of tackle, our jaws hit the floor. If you want more certainty, a fertility clinic might be able to help. You can probably order a kid with purple hair and glow-in-the-dark eyes if you want one, never mind a girl. But if I were you, I'd stop worrying. The only thing that really matters is that your new arrival is healthy.

> **Dear Dr Ozzy:**
> My wife's pregnant, and every time we leave the house, I get paranoid that her water might break. (What does this mean, anyway?) Would I have to deliver the baby myself?
> **Jason, Cardiff**

From what I understand – which ain't very much – babies grow inside a little watery sac, and when it bursts, the kid's ready to pop out. That's what it means when a pregnant woman's 'water breaks'. But there's no need to get all paranoid about it: even if it happens in public, it doesn't mean you have to deliver your son with a toilet plunger and a wooden spoon, or whatever it is you're imagining. All you need to do is drive your missus to the nearest hospital, sharpish. That's exactly what I had to do when my first daughter, Jessica, was born. There were a couple of problems – I didn't know how to drive and I'd been drinking all day. Apart from that, though, it was easy.

Dear Dr Ozzy:
My three-year-old son keeps being hit/kicked/bitten by the son of one of my friends. Even worse, my friend never does anything about it. What can I do?
Catherine, Washington, Tyne and Wear

As a parent, you've just gotta accept that some kids play rougher than others. That's all very well to say, mind you, until some brat whacks your little pumpkin over the back of the head with a wooden mallet. That happened to one of my kids at a playground in Staffordshire once. Before I even had time to think, I just turned around and chinned the other kid's dad. Looking back, I should have said something when the bullying first started – but I let it continue, getting worse and worse, until I finally blew my top. So I recommend you talk to your friend now – before she ain't your friend any more.

Dear Dr Ozzy:
Is it true that a cat might try to suffocate a newborn baby? My husband and I have just had our first child, and need to know if we should get rid of our eight-year-old moggy.
Victoria, Isle of Wight

I used to worry about the same thing. Basically, cats like sleeping in warm places, which is why they jump into cots. People also say they can smell the milk on a baby's breath. But you don't need to frog-march poor old Mr Moggins outside at dawn and shoot him. Just keep the door to your baby's room closed (as long as you've got a monitor) when the little one's asleep. Problem solved.

DR OZZY'S INCREDIBLY HELPFUL TIPS

Operating Instructions for Children

➕ Remember, babies aren't that much different from rock stars. They go crazy if they don't get enough to drink. They feel a lot better after they've thrown up on your new carpet. And they crap their pants more than once a day. Basically, the same as me during most of the eighties.

➕ Most pushchairs nowadays come with a beer holder and an ashtray. In an emergency, they can also be used to carry milk bottles and wet wipes.

➕ Don't even *think* about asking your own parents for advice about raising infants. At the age of sixty-two, I'm lucky if I can remember why I just walked into a room, never mind how I changed a fucking nappy in 1972. Mind you, I don't think I ever *did* change a nappy, so even if I could somehow go back in time, I still wouldn't have a clue. The best thing to do is work out it for yourself.

Dear Dr Ozzy:
I taught my three-year-old son a swear word for a
laugh and now I can't get him to stop saying it. I'm
mortified. What should I do?
Catherine, Aberdeen

Never, *ever*, swear in front of little kids: their brains are hard-wired to pick up on it – trust me. You can't get 'em to learn the alphabet to save your life, but they'll memorise every filthy word in the *Oxford English Dictionary* in a heartbeat. Fair enough, it might crack you up to hear a toddler effing and blinding, but it ain't so funny when you take your little blue-eyed angel to the in-laws' place and he says, 'Hello Grandma, you old c★★★.'

Dear Dr Ozzy:
My wife has signed up our son for football practice,
piano lessons and yoga. He's two. Is this insane?
Alex, Oxford

It sounds like he's ready to become prime minister. I mean, how old is David Cameron – four-and-a-half? Seriously, though, my advice would be to leave the kid alone. Buy him a cowboy suit. Get him a fucking Lego set. It's your missus who should sign up for something – *therapy*. A lot of parents these days just seem to be passing all of their insecurities on to their kids. I mean, piano lessons at two? Give me a break, man. What's next? Pilot training and deep-sea diving classes? We pile all this pressure on to these little people then wonder why they're burned out at nine. My advice is *slow down*.

Dear Dr Ozzy:
My four-year-old daughter is addicted to Angry Birds
on my iPad. Will this cause her any harm?
Scott, Los Angeles

I don't understand a single word of this question. Why do
you have birds on your iPad, and why are they pissed off?
The only thing I can think of is that this is some kind of
video game. If so, I don't think there's anything wrong with
your daughter playing it – in fact, it's probably good for
her – as long as there's a time limit. And, instead of snatch-
ing it away when her fifteen minutes are up – which will
just make her want it more – try distracting her with something else ... like the telly, *heh-heh-heh*.

Dear Dr Ozzy:
Did you think twice before vaccinating your kids, given
the controversy over vaccines and autism, or do you
think the fear is overblown by a few hysterical
Hollywood actor types?
Steve, Bognor

Hand on heart, I can't say I had anything to do with the
decision to vaccinate our kids – I was too busy vaccinating
myself with lakes of booze. But I was as freaked out as the
next parent when I heard all the talk a few years ago about
the shots being linked to autism. (The research turned out
to be bollocks, but a lot of people are still very concerned.)
The thing is, though, they don't stick needles in kids for
fun – they do it 'cos the diseases they prevent are fucking
horrendous. The only reason we don't realise how bad
things like whooping cough are is because they've been
virtually wiped out by the drugs. But here in California,

babies are now dying from it again, 'cos no one's getting their shots. To me, it doesn't make sense to expose your kids to things you *know* are dangerous just to avoid something that *might* be dangerous – no matter how suspicious you are of drugs companies and their dodgy ulterior motives. But everyone's different, and at the end of the day, you'll have to make the decision for yourself.

> **Dear Dr Ozzy:**
> I'm about to become the father of a baby boy. I'm not Jewish, but I'm wondering if I should get him circumcised – it just seems so much cleaner. What's your opinion?
> Alan, Leicester

I ain't Jewish, either, but I still got the old rusty scissor treatment – even though my two younger brothers didn't. I remember asking my mum what she was thinking, expecting some kind of logical explanation. Instead, she just went, 'Oh, it was the fashion.' The *fashion*? This was my most prized possession she was talking about, not a pair of bell-bottom jeans! Luckily, I didn't get any stick for the way I looked in the showers at school, mainly 'cos, in those days, the only showers we got were when it rained. But is it more hygienic? Well, given some of the very dark and smelly places I explored in the 1970s, I would say, 'Yes!' For most people, though, a bar of soap is probably just as effective.

> **Dear Dr Ozzy:**
> Every since our baby daughter was born, our three-year-old son has started to regress – making goo-goo, gah-gah noises, etc. Should we tell him to grow up and

act like a 'big boy', or go along with it while making
sure to give him more special attention?
Martha, Brixton

I feel very sad for the poor kid, 'cos he probably thinks his
mum and dad don't love him as much, now there's a brand-
new sibling in the house. As one of six Osbourne kids, I
can fully sympathise. Your son's feeling insecure, so I
wouldn't bollock him for making the baby noises. That
could just make it worse. A better idea would be to make
an extra special effort to give him some one-on-one attention: buy him an ice cream, take him to his favourite
park ... whatever. You just need to reassure him that he
hasn't been forgotten. If he keeps making the baby noises
after that, don't tell him to stop, just ask him gently to use
his 'big boy voice'. My guess is he'll grow out of it before
long.

Dear Dr Ozzy:
My wife wants to give our baby a pacifier. I'm putting up
a fight, because I think it'll be an impossible habit to
break. What's your expert medical opinion on this
matter?
David, Cornwall

If you're looking for some moral support, you've come to
the wrong guy. I once sent a private jet halfway across
America to go and get 'Baby' – my son Jack's teddy bear –
after we left it in a hotel room. That fucking blanket pretty
much ended up with its own security detail, we were so
scared of losing it. We've still got it today, in fact.
Meanwhile, my daughter Kelly had *two* pacifiers: one for
each hand. And if it's any reassurance, breaking the habit

wasn't difficult at all: one day, she just got bored of them, like kids do. Then it was straight on to the next big, exciting thing: her thumb.

> Dear Dr Ozzy:
> I was looking through my three-year-old son's locker at nursery school the other day and discovered that his best male friend – same age – had sent him a Valentine's card. What's more: the boy in question has two gay dads. I know we're supposed to be cool about this kind of thing nowadays, but I'm freaking out. Advice?
> Eric, Derby

It sounds like your problem isn't with the Valentine's Day card – the kid's three, so he ain't got a clue what it means, anyway – but with the two gay dads. I mean, would you be as freaked out if it were a boy with straight parents who'd sent it? Probably not. You'd probably even think it was cute. So you need to sit yourself down, remind yourself the world has changed a lot in the past few years, and get over it, to be honest.

ADVANCED PARENTING

> Dear Dr Ozzy:
> I found porn on my son's computer. What should I do?
> Liz, Los Angeles

I once found girlie magazines in my son's room, but what was I going to say to him? *I'm Ozzy fucking Osbourne.*

Luckily, you don't have that problem – although the answer to your question really depends on your son's age. If he's twelve, I don't think he should have unlimited access to a computer with an Internet connection. But if he's sixteen or older, I think it's completely normal for him to be interested in that kind of thing – as long as it ain't the really crazy, freaky stuff. The fact is, even most grown men like the occasional blue movie. I watch 'em on the road from time to time, 'cos it's better than picking up some groupie and having my balls turn green (not to mention the fact that I'm a happily married man). It can't hurt to talk to your kid about all this, though, if you can pluck up the courage. Better yet, have his father or a male friend strike up a conversation about it. Being open is usually the best way.

> **Dear Dr Ozzy:**
> My daughter has an enormous nose. I'm not going to lie: it's huge (although she has always looked beautiful to me). She says it's ruining her social life, and now she wants a nose job for her fourteenth birthday, which I'm told is normal these days. Advice?
> Zan, Florida

A lot of people will tell you that bullying makes you stronger and that you've gotta learn to take it if you want to get on in the world. The trouble is, when you're being called 'Big Nose' five hundred times a day because you've got Mount Everest stuck to your face, that advice ain't very fucking helpful. Like everything, the people who are so sure you've just got to put up with it don't have to handle the problem themselves. And kids can be incredibly cruel, y'know? Not only that, but teasing at school can mess you

up for the rest of your life. To this day, I'm still very insecure about my dyslexia, because I grew up being told that
I was stupid. So, look, people get birth-marks and other
harmless stuff removed all the time because of the way they
look. And it's really no different with a giant conk. Buy her
the nose job.

> Dear Dr Ozzy:
> My ten-year-old daughter borrowed my iPad without
> asking and found an explicit photograph of me and my
> girlfriend on it (I'm recently divorced from her mum).
> Now she won't speak to me – and I'm terrified of what
> my ex-wife is going to do. Help!
> Jerry, Milton Keynes

Adopt the brace position and prepare for the bollocking of
a lifetime! And to be honest, I ain't exactly overflowing
with sympathy for you myself. I mean, I'm useless when it
comes to iThis and iThat, but it doesn't take a fucking
genius to realise that you need to set a password before leaving a computer lying around, especially if there are kids in
the house. Mind you, taking those dirty pictures in the first
place wasn't the cleverest idea, either: it's meant to be you
who warns your kids about 'sexting', not the other way
around. The divorce only makes things worse, 'cos your
daughter was probably feeling weird and insecure about
your new relationship anyway. When she can finally look
you in the eye again, you need to have a heart-to-heart.
And while you ain't by any means in the clear yourself, you
need to explain to her that some things are private, and that
she shouldn't look at your stuff without permission. Point
out that when she gets older, she'll expect *you* to give *her*
some personal space, too.

Dear Dr Ozzy:
I suspect that my fifteen-year-old son is partaking in a bit of the old 'sweet leaf' – i.e., cannabis. Without damaging our good relationship, how can I deal with the, ahem, irony of it all?
Lonnie, Channel Islands

Here's what I always tell myself: we were all kids once, and when we were worried about being caught doing anything bad, we'd lie. When my father gave me the 'If I ever catch you smoking cigarettes' lecture, I still did it, but under wraps, so he wouldn't find out. So don't be militant about the drugs. Just come clean with your son, lay your cards on the table and say, 'Look, I know about the pot, and I'm *worried*.' Tell him that, unlike the dickhead who's been selling him weed, you love him unconditionally, and you're the best friend he'll ever have. It's better to be cool with your kids and have them talk to you than put up a brick wall and force them to sneak around behind it.

Dear Dr Ozzy:
I recently discovered that my thirteen-year-old daughter has been text-messaging racy photographs of herself to her boyfriend – 'sexting', as it's known. What on earth should I do?
Janice, North London

Get everyone in a room together – you, your daughter, your daughter's father, the boyfriend, the boyfriend's parents – and deliver a category-five bollocking. Ram it home to them how stupid it is. Then make absolutely sure that all copies of those pictures are destroyed. The thing you need to make clear is that you aren't angry with them for exploring their bodies – kids have always played 'doctors and nurses', after all – but because when you press 'send' on a phone or a computer, you lose control of that image for ever. All it takes is for some idiot to pick up the boyfriend's phone and forward the picture, and it could have gone around the world twice in a few hours. It might even end up on some websites you don't want to believe exist. And that's not to mention the embarrassment she'd suffer if any of her classmates got hold of it.

Dear Dr Ozzy:
My teenage son has started to spend hours alone in his bedroom. Now, when I go in there to clean, I notice crusty stains on the carpet. How can I tell him to use a tissue?
Anne, Edinburgh

Ask him if he's been making any Airfix planes recently, because you seem to be finding glue all over the place. Then tell him very nicely that you don't mind him making the models – it's perfectly normal at his age – but if he spills any more 'glue', he should wipe it up with a tissue. That's only polite. With any luck, he'll be so embarrassed, he'll never dirty the carpet again.

Dear Dr Ozzy:
My twenty-five-year-old daughter lives alone in London and has started to go on Internet dates. Is this safe? How can I get her to meet a man the old-fashioned way – i.e., offline?
Max, Hull

The Internet makes me glad I've got attention deficit disorder. Otherwise, I'd be as glued to the screen as everyone else, getting up to no good. But the truth is, times have changed, and I've heard a lot of stories about people meeting the love of their life online – so it can't be *all* bad. Besides, what's worse, arranging dates on a computer or getting picked up in a bar? The only thing I'd say to your daughter is, 'A guy can tell you anything he wants online, so don't believe everything you read. Plus, most guys want a bonk, not a wife.' Bearing that in mind, I hope she finds the right bloke.

Dear Dr Ozzy:
My son has taken up smoking to impress a new
girlfriend. How can I get him to stop?
Lauren, Staffordshire

I made the same mistake myself. I took some chick from Digbeth to the pictures when I was fourteen, and took along five fags and a penny book of matches to impress her. (You could smoke till you were blue in the face at the cinema in those days.) So there I was, sitting in this darkened room, puffing away, trying to be Jack the Lad, and suddenly I broke out in a cold sweat. *What the fuck's wrong with me?* I thought. Then I burped and tasted puke. I had to leg it to the bogs and lock myself in a stall while I coughed my guts up. I was *so* sick, man. Eventually, I dragged myself out of the exit and went straight home, throwing up the whole way. To this day, I don't know what happened to the girl. I wouldn't have touched another cigarette for as long as I lived if it hadn't been the 'normal' thing to do back then. So here's my suggestion: put your son off cigarettes by making him ill. Throw some fag ash on his cornflakes. Maybe that'll work.

Dear Dr Ozzy:
Like you, I'm covered in tattoos, but now my beautiful
seventeen-year-old daughter wants to get one. I'm
trying to talk her out of it, because I hate the way
tattoos look on young girls, but I feel like a hypocrite.
Please help.
Tony, Los Angeles

The trouble with tattoos is that they're addictive. I've known girls who start out with a little flower on their ankle, and three months later they've got an entire battle scene across their arse. When my own daughter got tattoos, I said to her, 'Look, fashions come and fashions go, and one day you might end up resenting what you did to your body when you were young.' It's one thing being young and beautiful with a tattoo, but another when you're a grandma with a floppy old dagger on your arm. I mean, there are times when even I wake up and look at the smiley face on my knee and think: What did I do *that* for? They hurt like crazy, too, when you first get 'em done. But I reckon the best idea is to tell your daughter that tattoos just aren't that special any more: *everyone* has 'em. If she really wants to be ahead of the pack, she should invest her money in one of those laser removal companies. They're gonna be making a fortune in a few years' time, when tattoos ain't the in thing any more.

Dear Dr Ozzy:
My son has failed (or near enough) all his GCSEs. The
only career option for him now is manual labour, but he
doesn't seem to care. How can I motivate him to do
better?
Brian, Cheshire

I was the same when I was a kid – and it wasn't until twenty years later that I found out it was all related to my dyslexia and ADHD (attention deficit hyperactivity disorder). Your son should get checked out for both of those things, 'cos there's a lot of help available now. The good news is that it's never too late to get an education these days, thanks to computers and the internet. When I was at school, three hundred years ago, it was different: when you were out on your ear, you were out on your ear. It was either the local factory or signing up as cannon fodder in the military. And they wouldn't even let me join the army. 'We want subjects, not *objects*,' they told me. Fortunately, I found something I loved with heavy metal. That's the secret, really: finding something you enjoy doing that can also pay the bills. At the end of the day, that matters more than any GCSE.

Dear Dr Ozzy:
My sixteen-year-old son says he's gay, but I think it's just the crowd he's hanging out with. Is there anything I can do – like hiring an escort, maybe – that might change his mind?
Neil, Brighton

To be honest with you, Neil, I take my hat off to your son for coming out to his old man at such a young age. That takes serious balls, and I very much doubt he'd go to all the bother if he wasn't a thousand million per cent sure. Hiring an escort for your son would just be an insult – not to mention illegal and more than a bit creepy. Don't do it, man. Tell your kid you love him and support him whether he's gay, straight, bi, trans, whatever. However awkward this might be for you, it'll feel like the end of the world for him if he thinks he's being rejected.

Dear Dr Ozzy:
Like you, I have a son from another marriage. The problem is that I find it hard to connect with him, because we've lived apart for years and we're both men, so we don't like to talk about our feelings. How can I get around this without it being embarrassing?
Nigel, Durham

This is a common problem with men. I remember trying to talk to my own dad. Every time I said anything to him, it was 'What now, Son?' or 'I'm busy, can we talk about this later?' But times have changed. Fathers aren't these distant, scary figures any more. Still, it can be difficult with a son you don't see very often, so I suggest going out for a quiet pint with him. As long as you don't get blasted, it might loosen you up a bit. At the very least, just show willingness to get together, and it'll happen naturally. Whatever you do, don't put it off. Feeling embarrassed is nothing compared to the regret of missing out on your kid's life.

Dear Dr Ozzy:
My fifteen-year-old daughter has started to dress in a way that would befit an employee of one of Peter Stringfellow's establishments. How do I explain to her that this will bring her the wrong kind of male attention without sounding like a boring old fart?
Bob, Sunderland

Unfortunately, all fathers who have girls have to go through this stage in their lives, and it ain't pleasant. Obviously, you've gotta talk to her (or, better yet, get her mother to talk to her). But there's only so far you can take it, 'cos at the end of the day she might just say, 'Okay, Mum and

Dad, you're right,' then get changed into her miniskirt and fishnets in the garden shed, or in the back of her best mate's car. The thing is, she probably *wants* male attention – maybe from one boy in particular – but she has to work out for herself how to tell the difference between the 'right' and the 'wrong' kind. As I always say to other parents, hold on to your drawers and hope she grows out of it.

SIBLINGS

Dear Dr Ozzy:
None of my siblings get along, but they all insist on getting together every year at Christmas. I'm already dreading it, but staying away isn't an option, unless I want a war with my mother. Any tips on getting through the day?
Mike, Cornwall

If you think *your* family is bad company at Christmas, you should have been at the Osbournes' during my drinking days. It wasn't exactly merry, put it that way: by the end of the day, I'd be half-naked, covered in cranberry sauce, and throwing bricks at people. Then there was the year I bought two twenty-eight-gallon barrels of beer – bitter and mild – and set them up in my home studio. I got through both of 'em in less than a week. It got to the point where I was getting up in the night to use the toilet, and having a quick pint on my way back to bed. My ex-wife would find me each morning passed out in the slops. To answer your question, though: if I were you, I'd use the two rules of family gatherings – arrive early and leave early. I understand you've got to show your face, but there's nothing to stop you limiting the torture as much as possible.

> **Dear Dr Ozzy:**
> My dad is close to having a nervous breakdown over my twenty-five-year-old sister's choice of boyfriend. He's an illegal immigrant and a heavy dope smoker with (I'm not kidding) a tattoo of a pork chop and two chicken drumsticks on his chest. What can I do to put her off him?
> Chaz, Birmingham

If you want someone to do something, tell them *not* to do it. This guy could be an axe-murderer, but if you say to your sister, 'Look, he doesn't fit the mould,' (or if you call Immigration), she might just run off with him. You shouldn't lie, though, and nor should your old man: if your sister asks for approval, you should both tell her exactly what you think. I've had all sorts come into my house over the years to see my girls . . . although most of the time *they* don't approve of *me*, not the other way round. My guess is that eventually your sister will say to herself, 'What am I doing with this pork chop dickhead?' In the meantime, tell your dad to hold on, this stage will pass.

> **Dear Dr Ozzy:**
> My brother is thirty going on thirteen. He has never lived on his own, and my parents won't kick him out. What can I say/do to get him to pull his head out of his backside and grow up?
> Sara, Texas

When I was growing up in England, this problem was always the other way round – parents wanted their kids to look after them. It was the only reason why most people had kids in the first place. These days, I know grown men in their fifties who are still living with their folks. It's fucking unbelievable, man. I mean, what happens when you want to bring a girl home to give her a good old seeing to, and your mum comes in halfway through to bring you a cup of tea and a sandwich? It doesn't look very smooth, does it? At the end of the day, though, people do what they want to do, and there ain't much you can say to stop 'em. Especially brothers. Maybe you should just buy yours a DVD of *The Forty-Year-Old Virgin* to give him a glimpse of his future.

> **Dear Dr Ozzy:**
> My wife's brother-in-law is a handyman/contractor, so we feel obliged to use him for all our jobs around the house. The problem is he's useless, and he complains all the time. How can we get ourselves out of this awkward situation? (My wife sees her sister every day, so she doesn't want any tension or weirdness.)
> Billy, Scarborough

If you can write to Dr Ozzy about this, your missus can surely have a quiet word with her sister. Not, 'Your husband's an incompetent, whingeing arsehole,' but something along the lines of, 'Look, our two husbands have been butting heads on this DIY project, and I'm worried that if they keep at it they might fall out. I'd really hate that to happen, so why don't we tell 'em to take a break from working together on the house for a while?' The alternative is just to put up with it. But in my experience of having renovated half the Western Hemisphere with Sharon, people get very stressed out during construction work, so at some point voices will be raised ... or worse.

SPOUSES & IN-LAWS

Dear Dr Ozzy:
I have three small kids and would love to live nearer my
mum so she can help out. My husband is refusing to
move, however, based on the advice of his late father
'never to live in the same town as your mother-in-law'.
How can I change his mind?
Sonia, Paris

It's one thing saying, 'I married *you*, not your mum' when
you're footloose and fancy free, but it's quite another when
you've got three little kids, which can feel like having three
full-time jobs sometimes. If your husband continues to put
his foot down, I think it's perfectly reasonable for you to say
to him, 'Okay, either you need to chip in more with the
work around the house or you need to earn more money
so we can afford some extra help.' Faced with a choice
between losing his free time or his beer money, living a bit
closer to your mum might suddenly seem like a brilliant
idea.

Dear Dr Ozzy:
My mother-in-law is the world's worst cook. How can I
avoid eating her food without offending her?
Stephanie, Durham

Get a dog. That way, you can look like a hero by filling up
your plate and then coming back for more . . . while passing down handfuls of lumpy mashed potato to your
four-legged friend under the table. Just don't get a dog that's

too big: having a ten-stone Rottweiler burping and slobbering by your feet's gonna be a bit of a giveaway, especially
if he farts. Another trick is to stuff the food in your pocket.
I once managed to fit all three courses of one of Sharon's
dinners into my coat. The only problem was that I forgot all
about it, so when she took a trip to the dry-cleaner's a few
months later, she found my stash of rock-hard dumplings.
Most of 'em ended up being thrown at my head.

> **Dear Dr Ozzy:**
> My wife has suddenly started going to a local 'happy
> clappy' church. I'm not religious at all, and, to be
> honest, I find it all very disturbing. Is it possible to have
> a marriage where one person is an atheist and the
> other is a devout Christian?
> Oliver, Darlington

Some people turn to God like others turn to cocaine –
usually 'cos there's something missing in their lives. I had a
very good friend who was an addict for years, gave it up,
and instantly became a Jesus-freak. It was like he swapped
one addiction for the other. Talk to your wife about it. See
if you can find out what's making her so intense all of a
sudden. But if she continues this way, there's gonna be a
blow-up at some point, mark my words. Evangelists are
supposed to evangelise, so eventually she's gonna be on
your case about the 'good news'. And that'll be very bad
news for you. (After this question was published, I received
an e-mail from a guy called Paul, who said his Catholic
mum and atheist dad had been together for thirty years.
'The bottom line is if they have love and respect for each
other,' he told me. 'If not, then that's where the problems
start, irrespective of religious persuasion.')

Dear Dr Ozzy:
My partner is divorced and has three kids who don't live with us. The trouble is he never stops talking about them. He even talks to me about his bloody ex-wife! It's driving me mad, but I'm afraid to mention it, in case he thinks I'm narrow-minded.
Julia, London

I've had first-hand experience of this problem, and it's a tough one. At one point I was spending so much time juggling between my first wife, Thelma, and my second wife, Sharon, that I'd come home and call the missus 'Tharon' – which earned me more than a few black eyes, believe me. Over in California, you hear of these weird families where they've all divorced and remarried but remained friends. But that's gotta be pretty fucked up. I mean, we're all human. It sounds to me like you've started to feel a bit like the booby prize when it comes to your bloke. My advice would be to talk to him about it, but do it in a way that doesn't sound like you're having a go. Put yourself in his shoes: ask yourself what it would be like if you had a little boy or girl from another marriage, and how much you'd love them and want to stay in touch. But then explain to him that you have feelings, too, and that you need to know how you fit into his world.

Dear Dr Ozzy:
My mother-in-law complains to me – in detail – about how my father-in-law fails to satisfy her in bed. What sort of brain eraser do you recommend? (I'm tempted by the Smith & Wesson method.)
Nina, Texas

As far as my kids are concerned, having sex over the age of forty-five should be illegal. Never in a million years would I talk to them directly – never mind their partners – about giving one to their mum (although if they read this book they ain't gonna have much choice). I mean, what's wrong with this woman? No one in their right mind wants to think about their father-in-law's one-eyed wonder, or how bad he is at swinging it between the sheets. I recommend changing the subject whenever she brings it up ... or buying ear-plugs.

> **Dear Dr Ozzy:**
> My parents don't get along with each other any more, but they're so old now – late sixties and early seventies – that they don't want to divorce and end up living alone. But their unhappiness with each other is making everyone around them miserable, too. Any words of wisdom?
> Catherine, Boston

It's not what they should do, it's what *you* should do. Call a family meeting. I do this all the time when something's bothering me. Tell your folks that their bickering is getting everyone down, and that it's reaching the point where it's causing you so much anxiety that you don't even want to spend time with them any more – which makes you sad, 'cos you love them both very much. If they still can't resolve their problems after that, ask if they can at least make an effort to be civil to each other while you're around.

> **Dear Dr Ozzy:**
> My wife gets very aggressive during her 'time of the month', but if I point this out, she gets even angrier. What can I do about this?
> Gary, London

Four words that a married man should never say to his wife, especially during an argument: 'time of the month'. It's the atomic bomb option, and the bomb's only ever gonna land in one place: on your fucking head. Personally, I have a lot of sympathy for women when it comes to the TOTM – it must be awful. My advice to you, Gary, is simply to get out of the house if you suspect that's what's putting your missus in a bad mood. As anyone in the army will tell you, it's harder to hit a moving target.

> **Dear Dr Ozzy:**
> I want to propose to my girlfriend. The trouble is her father died ten years ago, and she doesn't really like her stepfather. Do I need to ask his permission?
> Ted, Stevenage

No. But if you want to keep the peace, why not ask the mother and the stepfather at the same time? It's never a bad idea to suck up to the in-laws, 'cos if you're anything like me, at some point you're gonna need all the goodwill you can get.

> **Dear Dr Ozzy:**
> I'm convinced my husband has fallen in love with one of his colleagues, but I don't think he's having an affair – yet. Should I do nothing or confront him? I'd prefer it if he had a one-night stand than a close emotional relationship with another woman.
> Joan, Bristol

Unless you have convincing evidence that something dodgy's going on, I'd leave it alone. Otherwise, your husband could end up saying to himself, 'Well, she thinks I'm messing around anyway, so why not go for it?' Or you could make him defensive, then he might start to lie and you'll have a big wedge between you. The absolute last thing you want to do is make it you versus them, 'cos that'll just make 'em closer. One sneaky tactic you could use is to befriend this woman and start hanging out with her all the time – the old 'keep your enemies closer' game. Not that Sharon would ever do that. If she ever suspected anything, she'd be round the other woman's house in a heartbeat, breathing fire all over the place, and scaring the living shit out of her.

> **Dear Dr Ozzy:**
> **This will make me sound like a chauvinistic pig, but I hate the fact that my wife earns far more than me. It's not like she brags, but it's driving me insane that she pays for everything, from the nanny to our family car. How can I consider myself a 'real man'?**
> **Jasper, Surrey**

I know exactly how you feel. When I first started seeing Sharon, I was the smelly guy who'd pissed away all his money and been fired by his band, and she was the one with diamonds and fur whose dad was a multi-millionaire. It made me feel terrible. In fact, I think it would make any man feel terrible, unless he was some kind of gigolo who preyed on loaded women. It might be an old-fashioned way of looking at the world, but I don't think there's anything wrong with wanting to provide for your family. If that ain't an option, though, you just need to make sure the missus knows you're grateful – maybe by cooking dinner, doing the dishes, giving her foot massages, etc. *Don't* do what I did and steal a bunch of flowers from the nearest graveyard to give to her. It seemed like a good idea at the time, but it soon backfired when she realised there was a card attached. She thought it was gonna to be a romantic poem or something. Instead it said, 'In loving memory of our dearest Harry.'

> Dear Dr Ozzy:
> My wife insists on going to therapy every week, but as the earner in the family, I get lumped with the bills. Now the therapist is telling her she needs an expensive holiday – and that she should stand up to me more on 'financial issues'! So I'm paying someone to make me poorer and ruin my marriage. What should I do?
> Steven, Norwich

I've been in a similar situation myself, and there's an easy solution: suggest to the missus that you go along to one of her sessions. Then you can say to the therapist in person, 'Look, I resent the fact that I'm forking out good cash to help my wife, and all you're doing is poisoning her against me.' Or you could just chin the guy and say, 'Analyse *that*.' Seriously, though, you've gotta give your side of the story. Therapists aren't superhuman – they're just paid to listen (and sometimes make suggestions). If your wife refuses to let you go with her, it might be time to get suspicious. She could be using her weekly sessions as a cover for something else, possibly involving the gardener.

Dr Ozzy's Trivia Quiz:
Flesh & Blood

*Find the answers – and add up
your score – on page 280*

*Find the answers – and add up
your score – on page 280*

1. Which well-known historic person was sold to human traffickers by his family when he was a kid?

a) Martin Luther King
b) Joseph (from the Bible)
c) Oliver Cromwell

2. What (allegedly) is the highest number of babies ever born to one woman?

a) 71
b) 102
c) 69

3. In 2010, a woman in New Mexico, USA, did *what* to her daughter-in-law during a fight?

a) Ripped off her nipple
b) Pushed her out of a tenth-floor window
c) Tattooed 'FOR SALE' on her forehead

4. According to therapists, what is the secret to a successful marriage?

a) Using flattery and persuasion
b) A bonk every other day
c) Being a total loser

5. How old was the youngest (confirmed) mother in medical history?

a) Seven
b) Six
c) Five

5

Surgery – Not Just for the Professionals

If You Want Something Done ... Do It Yourself

Okay, before we start this chapter, I don't want anyone getting the wrong idea. I'm not suggesting you should buy a hacksaw, a pair of barbecue tongs and a tube of SuperGlue, then set about removing one of your kidneys. If something's bothering you, and you've got any choice in the matter, *go to a fucking doctor* – a real one, not Dr Ozzy – instead of trying to fix the problem yourself. Especially if it involves chopping something off, taking something out, or enlarging anything.

Sometimes, though, doing it yourself is the only way to go. Like that guy who went hiking in Utah, got stuck under a rock, and had to chop off his own arm. If he hadn't been willing to get his hands dirty, he'd still be under that rock today. Then there was the famous case of that woman in Mexico who went into labour when she was all alone in the middle of nowhere. (She lived halfway up a mountain and her husband was at the pub.) She didn't want to risk going through labour, 'cos her last baby had been stillborn, so she necked half a bottle of rubbing alcohol, got out the kitchen knife, and gave herself a C-section before passing out. The kid was fine ... although I suppose he had a bit of a hangover in the morning.★

Obviously, it's unlikely you'll ever find yourself in such a heavy-duty situation. On the off-chance, though, I recommend tearing out the next few pages and keeping 'em with you at all times.

Dear Dr Ozzy:
I think my arm is broken, but I don't have health insurance, and I don't want to end up getting a bill for thousands of dollars from a hospital emergency room.
Is there a fail-safe (and painless) way to make your own plaster cast?
Stephen, Florida

Okay, Stephen, this is what you have to do: get yourself down to the local Wal-Mart and buy three paper cups, some sticky-backed plastic, a pen, four knitting needles and a ball of string. You'll also need a lemon, some ice and a tube of toothpaste. Oh, and a bag of cement mix. Lay it all out on the kitchen table. Take a deep breath. Then GO TO A DOCTOR. Honestly, are you fucking *mad*? Even if you don't have any dough, the ER will still treat you, and you can deal with the debt-collectors later. Trust me, your arm is going to be a lot more useful than any cash you might spend.

★ This is totally fucking true! The mum's name was Ines Ramirex Perez, and she had the baby on 5 March 2000 (according to the Associated Press).

Dear Dr Ozzy:
If I ever had to remove my own leg in an emergency
(say I was trapped under something heavy while a long
way from home, as in the movie *127 Hours*), how
difficult would it be?
Jay, Los Angeles

Depends. If you had a chainsaw handy, it wouldn't be difficult at all – apart from the screaming agony part. Also, it goes without saying that you'd have to be pretty fucking sure there were no other options before you went all-in. The last thing you'd want would be to go to all the bother of amputating your own leg, only for ten fire engines to pull up three minutes later. In terms of the technicalities, I can only tell you what I saw on *127 Hours*: you need to make a tourniquet; saw through the skin, flesh and muscle; find a way to break the bone (or bones); then snip the tendons. Then you've gotta find help before dying of blood loss or infection. In other words, it's best avoided, if at all possible.

DR OZZY'S INSANE-BUT-TRUE STORIES

DIY Surgery – What *Not* To Try

- Self-circumcision with a pair of old nail clippers. A bloke in Hertfordshire tried this in 2009 and ended up in A & E with a plaster cast on his knob. 'This is something we would advise men *never* to attempt,' said the hospital. No fucking shit, man.

- Gastric bypass operation using a kit you bought on Amazon. This ain't a joke: a company in America was selling 'Laparoscopic Gastric Bypass Kits' on the internet until recently. It was all a big mistake, apparently: the kit was supposed to be available only to hospitals. Still, it got thirty-eight 'user reviews' – all of 'em from people taking the piss.

- Brain surgery. A bit of an obvious one this, I would have thought – but not to a chick in Gloucester who drilled a hole in her own head while standing in front of a mirror (with a video camera running), 'cos she'd been told it might cure 'tiredness'. It all went well apart from the fact that she put a big fucking hole in her head. And I've no idea how much brain damage she did – after all, there can't have been much grey matter there to begin with. Afterwards, she insisted she felt much better.

- Laser eyesight correction. The main problem with zapping your own eyeballs is that you need your eyes to make sure you're pointing the laser in the right direction. It's also pretty hard to get your hands on a reliable laser, unless you live in a volcano and answer to the name 'Ernst Stavro Blofeld'. The one in your old CD player certainly ain't gonna do much good.

Dear Dr Ozzy:
I want to look like a celebrity but can't afford to get my acne scars removed by a surgeon. If I buy my own silicone on the Internet, could I simply treat the scars myself? (I've seen how doctors on reality TV shows do the injections.)
Jaynie, London

No, no, and fuck no. A million times NO. I saw Neil Armstrong land on the moon on the telly, but that doesn't mean I could pilot the Mars Rover, does it? I've heard terrible stories about people buying the wrong kind of silicone – like the stuff they put in car engines – and shooting themselves up with it, only to end up looking like Freddy Krueger from *Nightmare on Elm Street*. The worst thing is that you can't just leave it in there: someone has to cut your face open and get it out. To be honest, though, I'm not even sure your acne scars are the real problem. If you're obsessed enough about your looks that you're willing to stick a needle in yourself, there might be something else going on. I would recommend talking to a therapist, 'cos it might be that you're suffering from some kind of negative body image disorder. I ain't got anything against plastic surgery – I've had it done myself, and so has my wife – but sometimes people get way too hung up on the stuff.

Dear Dr Ozzy:
I crushed my finger between two heavy steel pipes.
Now it's swollen and black. Do you think it's broken?
Phil, Essex

This question isn't as stupid as it sounds, 'cos I once broke my tibia – my shin bone – and didn't realise it for weeks. I thought it was just bruised. Mind you, I was so blasted all the time, you could have taken a chainsaw to my right arm and I probably wouldn't have noticed. In fact, I broke my tibia in the first place because I was off my nut and fell down a flight of stairs. The other problem was that no one ever used to listen to me when I complained about breaking something, because they all knew I used it as an excuse to get my hands on some pills so I could get even more out of my skull. I was like the boy who cried wolf, y'know? Especially when we were in America. I mean, you can't go to a doctor in the States for *anything* without coming away with a bottle of pills. I used to turn up at appointments with a fucking shopping trolley. And in my darkest days, I used to *try* to injure myself to get pills. Which brings me back to the question: if you're asking me if your finger's broken, you're obviously not the kind of person who tries to scam your GP, so, if I were you, I'd get it X-rayed. Or you could just try to play a couple of games of snooker. You'll know if it's broken pretty fast if you do that.

> **Dear Dr Ozzy:**
> I have a corn on my right foot, and after a lot of consideration, I'm thinking of trimming it myself. Are there any risks I should know about?
> Gian, Frosinone, Italy

Don't do it, man. Seriously. I had a hairdresser once who got some kind of growth on his foot, so he dealt with it himself, forgot about it for years, then found out – too late – that it was cancer. The other thing you've gotta bear in mind is that your entire body is weighing down on that foot for most of the day, so if things go wrong in that area, there might be consequences you can't even imagine. I mean, if you had a blow-out on your car, would you get out your bicycle repair kit, glue the little patch over the hole, then head out on the motorway? No, you wouldn't. So get yourself to your GP or, better yet, a chiropodist.

> **Dear Dr Ozzy:**
> Is it true that a Russian GP stationed in Antarctica removed his own appendix, spent only a fortnight

**recovering, then carried on with his work? Could
anyone perform a self-appendectomy if there was no
other help available?**
Gillian, Spain

I got someone to look this up for me, and, as mind-blowing as it sounds, it's absolutely true. It ain't the only case, either. A doctor in America took out his own appendix just to prove that his anaesthetic worked. (It's a good job the guy wasn't selling guns for a living – he might have shot himself in the head to prove his bullets worked.) But just because a few nutters have managed to slice themselves open and lived to tell the tale, that doesn't mean anyone else should try it. Unless you've got a set of mirrors handy, some very sharp knives, a bag of hardcore antibiotics and a pair of balls the size of Mount Rushmore, you'd be better off using your energy to find medical attention before you start digging around in your own abdomen. I mean, could you honestly say you even know what your appendix looks like? Knowing me, I'd end up cutting out a lung instead.

Dr Ozzy's Trivia Quiz:
Under The Knife

*Find the answers – and tote up
your score – on page 281*

1. **Doctors have fucked up and made which of these
   horrendous medical errors?**
   a) Amputating the wrong leg
   b) Bifurcation (which left the patient with a forked tongue)
   c) Transplanting the wrong heart and lungs

2. **Which of these DIY cosmetic surgeries did people
   attempt?**
   a) A nose job with a chisel and a chicken bone
   b) Double-chin surgery with a bread knife and a vacuum
      cleaner
   c) Lip augmentation with an injection of sexual lubricant

3. **What does 'auto-enucleation' mean?**
   a) Deliberately exposing yourself to radiation
   b) Gouging out your own eyes
   c) When your body rejects an anaesthetic

4. In medieval times, who did you go to for surgery?

a) A barber
b) A blacksmith
c) A carpenter

5. Which of these famous medical cases resulted in death?

a) The man who removed his own pacemaker
b) The man who deliberately cycled into the back of a lorry to fracture his jaw, so it could be reset in a 'more attractive' way
c) The woman who tried to give herself liposuction by cutting her thighs and squeezing out the fat

6

General Practice

Dr Ozzy's A-to-Z of Uncommon Complaints

Every day, people write to me about the craziest shit you've ever heard in your life. A lot of the questions are so far-out that it's impossible to sort them into any normal categories. That's why I've put all the wacky stuff in this chapter and listed it alphabetically – so if you swallow a tennis ball, get a screwdriver stuck in your right ear, or start vomiting through your eyeballs, all you've gotta do is look under the right letter and hope you find the answer. Personally, I wish I'd had a guide like this for myself over the years. It would have come in very handy when my right leg started to dance by itself (look under 'J' for 'Jimmy Legs'), or when I accidentally ate a bumble bee on the way to the pub (see 'F' for 'Flies & Other Insects (Swallowed)'). You'll also find some 'Surgery Noticeboard' announcements following between the Q&As: we print these in the *Sunday Times Magazine* whenever we get a ton of e-mails on one subject. As a fake newspaper doctor with fuck-all qualifications, I'm always happy to pass along other people's advice.

A.

Animals (Effect on Mood)

Dear Dr Ozzy:
My dog, Clive (a Labrador), seems awfully glum, to the point where it's beginning to get me down. Could he be suffering from doggie depression? If so, what can I do about it?
Amy, Lille, France

Doggie Prozac – ask your vet about it. Personally, the only doggie depression I've ever experienced is the feeling I get after one of my four-legged friends takes a dump behind the sofa.

Animals (Effect on Sleep)

Dear Dr Ozzy:
Every night I go to bed with my dog, Ozzy (named after you), but wake up at 4 a.m. I really want to stay in bed longer, but no matter what I do, I can't get back to sleep. Is this something to do with Ozzy, do you think? Please help, it's driving me crazy.
Sammy (no address given)

I don't see how one dog could be much of an issue – I go to bed with seventeen dogs, plus about twenty mobile phones, and the wife. To me, it sounds more like you've got a sleep disorder. I've had the same problem for years, so I got someone to come over to the house one evening, put all these electrode things on my head, hook them up to a computer, and see what was going on in my brain. He was up all night, this guy, twiddling his knobs and studying his graphs. He must be a raging insomniac himself. When the results came back, my doc put me on a mild anti-depressant, which helps me nod off easier. It beats sleeping pills. Or whacking myself on the head with a mallet.

B.

Brain (Use of)

Dear Dr Ozzy:
Is it true that humans use only 10 per cent of their brains, or is this just another of those stupid myths?
Andrew, Kent

I fucking hope that ain't the case, 'cos I've only got about 10 per cent of my brain *left*. By your reckoning, that means I'm running on about 1 per cent these days. Actually . . . that explains a lot.

Breath (Offensive)

Dear Dr Ozzy:
My breath is really bad – to the point where I can't talk to people who are close to me. I'm a student here in

Ghana, and I find it difficult even just to say 'Hello' to
friends on campus, because I just don't want to
embarrass myself. Please, Dr Ozzy, I need your help.
Emmanuel, Ghana

A long time ago, I made a pact with my wife: if my breath
is bad, she has to tell me – and vice versa. Obviously, no one
needs to break the news to *you*, Emmanuel. By the sound of
it, when you open your mouth, the sun gags. My guess is
that the problem is caused by one of two things: something
very nasty in your gut or gum disease. If I were you, my first
stop would be a dentist – although you might want to give
her some advance warning, so she can put on a rubber suit
and face mask, and light a few candles around the room first.
In the meantime, try Euthymol, an old English brand of
toothpaste, which makes you feel like you just gargled with
petrol and lit a match. Also buy some ultra-strength mouthwash, like Listerine, and get yourself a tongue scraper.

Burping (Potential Side-Effects of)

Dear Dr Ozzy:
A friend told me that burping too hard can rip a hole in
your stomach. Is this true?
Anna (twelve years old),
Long Island, New York

Total bollocks. I wouldn't have any stomach left if that were
the case. In fact, I once saw a bloke on telly who could talk
and burp at the same time. I tried to do it myself once, but
ended up puking into Sharon's handbag. Lesson: some
things are best left to the professionals.

Bedbugs

Dear Dr Ozzy:
My husband and I have developed such a paralysing
fear of bedbugs that we've become like prisoners in our
own home. How can we get over our paranoia?
Tara, West Village, New York

I've never had a problem with bedbugs – probably 'cos they take one sip of my blood and drop dead from all the toxic shit in there. But I understand your concern: no one wants to wake up with a thousand little red bite marks on their ball-sack. Just bear in mind that bedbugs aren't all that serious. I'm about to go to South America, for example, and I'm told they have these 'kissing spiders' that crawl up your body and on to your face, squat over your lips, secrete an anaesthetic, suck out the blood, take a dump, then scamper back to their holes. But that's not the worst part: the spider crap contains a kind of bacteria that literally eats your heart out. I'm so freaked out about it, I'm probably gonna spend the whole tour sleeping in a sealed fucking Ziploc bag.

C.

Cancer (Coping With)

Dear Dr Ozzy:
In the past five years, I've had two hip operations,
throat cancer and now a serious heart problem. As a

result of chemo- and radiotherapy, I can eat only liquid
food through a syringe into my stomach, and sex is
impossible because of the beta blockers I take for my
ticker. Thankfully, I can still drink beer, but otherwise
I'm rapidly losing my sense of humour, which isn't like
me. How can I cheer myself up?
Charlie (sixty-five years old), Devon

This is one of the reasons why medical marijuana ain't nec-
essarily such a bad idea. I mean, anyone who reads 'Ask Dr
Ozzy' on a regular basis knows that I usually tell people to
steer clear of weed 'cos you never know how strong it is,
or how you'll react to it (never mind that it's illegal). But in
Los Angeles, a lot of people with heavy-duty medical problems say that prescription pot helps them with everything
from muscle pain to getting back their appetite. My advice
is to talk to your doctor, keep drinking the beer, and try to
find something – *anything* – else that gives you a break from
the discomfort. It sounds like you've had some rotten luck,
Charlie, and I wish you all the best.

Chewing Gum (Ingested)

Dear Dr Ozzy:
I just swallowed a piece of chewing gum. Is it true this
will take seven years to pass through my system?
Frank, Portsmouth

That can't be true, because if it was I'd be half-human, half-
spearmint by now.

Cruise Ships (Downsides of)

Dear Dr Ozzy:
My wife wants to go on an expensive cruise, but I'm afraid of getting food poisoning, falling overboard or being seasick. Am I being paranoid?
Tyler, Atlanta

No, you ain't. I took the *QE2* to America once with Sharon, 'cos she was pregnant and couldn't fly. I was so out of my fucking mind with boredom, it would have been a *relief* to fall overboard. In the end, I begged the ship's doc to give me something to knock me out. When I finally woke up in New York, Sharon was so angry, she tried to push me through one of the portholes. I've never been on a cruise ship since.

Crying (During Urination)

Dear Dr Ozzy:
I cry when I urinate. Tears literally stream from my eyes, like I'm peeling an onion. It's not painful or anything, but I'm worried I have a rare disease. What's your expert advice?
Pierre, Barcelona

No offence, Pierre, but this is really fucking weird. Here's my prescription: 1) Keep a box of tissues by the bog; and 2) Get a second opinion, ideally from someone whose name ain't Ozzy Osbourne.

D.

Death (Stress Related to)

Dear Dr Ozzy:
My fiancé of two years – a wealthy Arab man – has been told he has terminal cancer. After trying to ignore the subject, I asked about his will (I'm no longer working because of the economic crisis). He told me that he's giving everything to charity because he hates his family. When I asked about me, he said I would get nothing either. I told him I was hurt, but he said he was more hurt, because he's dying and I asked him for money. (I did feel like a jerk for asking, but I need a place to live.) Who's in the right?
Margaret, London

It sounds to me like your fiancé is angry about dying – it's hard to blame him – and he's lashing out. But you shouldn't feel like a jerk, either. I mean, if the bloke's giving all his money away to his cocker spaniel (or whatever his favourite charity is), who's going to pay for his funeral? Is he happy to think he'll be tossed into some municipal pit with a cardboard headstone? And if he cared about you enough to get engaged, why does he want you out on the street? Fair enough, he doesn't have to give you every last penny he earned during his lifetime, but sorting out your digs for a year or two so you can get back on your feet ain't too much to ask. I can't stress enough that people need to get these things down in writing early on, before a situation like this comes up. It's normal to want to put anything related to death on the back-burner, but *everyone* needs a will. It ain't very nice talking about the final curtain, but it's a lot worse to have the conversation when you're coping with a tragedy.

Dentistry (Basic Techniques)

Dear Dr Ozzy:
I've been getting a lot of severe headaches recently and have been told that they could be caused by teeth-grinding. Is it possible to grind your teeth without knowing it?
Jennifer, Northumberland

You and I have exactly the same problem. I started getting these really bad headaches a few weeks ago. Being a hypochondriac, I thought: Right, that's it, I've got a brain tumour. I was one stage away from buying myself a casket when my GP told me that I needed to see a dentist, not an oncologist. So that's what I did, and now I've got these little rubber things to put over my teeth at night, to stop me grinding them in my sleep – which, to answer your question, is supposedly very common. I don't wear them half the time, though, 'cos it's a major ball-ache putting them in. I'd rather take an aspirin.

Dear Dr Ozzy:
If I rinse my mouth out with kettle descaler, will it get rid of my plaque? I ask because my dental hygienist charges fifty quid a time to do the same thing, and it's getting expensive.
Peter, Lowestoft

If you think fifty quid is expensive for a scrape and polish, just see how much they charge the idiot who comes in with no teeth 'cos he gargled with sodium tripolyphosphate. They'll still be sending you bills when you're six feet under. In fact, this reminds me of the time one of my good friends tried to cure a rash on his honourable gentleman with a bottle of Domestos, 'cos he didn't want to have to admit to his family GP that he'd been unfaithful to his wife. Needless to say, his missus found out soon enough, 'cos he spent the next month in hospital, screaming in pain.

> **Dear Dr Ozzy:**
> You and your lovely wife both have great teeth . . . so white! What I'd like to know is would you recommend using shop-bought whitening agents? As a smoker who drinks too much coffee, I'm badly in need of a non-celebrity solution.
> **Freda, Milton Keynes**

I hate to break it to you, Freda, but my choppers ain't real. All my teeth are screwed in: for cleaning, they just unscrew 'em and give 'em a good polish. They ain't falsies, though – they're implants. I started out with caps, which means they file down your teeth to posts and cement crowns on top of them. But then the posts rotted away, so they gave me implants, which are attached to my jaws with titanium screws. If I had my real teeth, I'd look like Herman Munster's ugly brother. I think growing up in Britain is partly to blame – I mean, we're not exactly renowned for our great teeth, are we? Even Harley Street dentists aren't that good. I went to a bloke who does the royals' teeth once, and I came out of the place looking like a racehorse. But the biggest problem for me was being a drug addict: it kills all your calcium, which is what keeps your mouth healthy. Getting back to your question, though: I don't have a clue about whitening agents, but it can't do any harm to give them a go, can it? As for a 'non-celebrity solution', the good news is that you don't have to be famous to see a dentist in Beverly Hills. You do need a ton of dough, though.

Doctors (Issues Regarding)

Dear Dr Ozzy:
Do you think people should be allowed to rate their doctors on the internet, like they can rate albums? Or do you think the medical profession is too important to be subjected to the kind of abuse you got in 1970 for the first Black Sabbath LP?
Sally, Glasgow

Honestly? I don't know. I mean, my GP might give me a drug for something, and I might get better with no side-effects. But another person might get exactly the same treatment, and his head might swell up to ten times its normal size. So would it be fair if the guy with the massive head gave the doc a bad review? Probably not. Then again, if you were gonna have heart surgery, and the reviews told you that your surgeon's last ten patients had all croaked it on the operating table, you'd want to know. But the way I see it, a doctor spends years and serious amounts of dough to become qualified to make life-or-death decisions, so it ain't fair if one person with a bee up their arse can ruin his career with a review that takes three seconds to write.

Dear Dr Ozzy:
Like you, I've always been a bit of a hypochondriac.
However, for the past twenty-odd years (since my
parents died, and my newborn son needed heart
surgery) I've had a phobia of anything to do with
doctors. I avoid them as long as the pain doesn't
become unbearable. My head tells me that I should
take your advice and benefit from modern medicine,
but unfortunately the coward in me is stronger. Any
advice?
Christine, Germany

If you're too afraid to go to the doctor 'cos it brings back
painful memories – or 'cos you're worried that you'll get
bad news – there's only one solution: *don't go.* Simple as
that. Go to the pub instead. At the end of the day,
Christine, only you can make the decision. The thing is,
though, if you're afraid of getting bad news, isn't it better
to get it sooner rather than later? The only reason my wife
is still alive is because she got bad news *early.* That meant
she was able to get to her cancer before it spread and killed
her. Speaking for myself, if I don't go to the doctor on a
regular basis, I just drive myself nuts about every little
twinge and ache. It sounds like you're already worrying
yourself sick, too. So why not take a deep breath and make
an appointment?

Dribble (Excessive)

Dear Dr Ozzy:
I've started to dribble at night while asleep, meaning I
wake up every morning to an unpleasantly damp pillow.

Is this normal at my age (early sixties, like you), and is
there a cure?
John, Essex

Believe me, there are much worse ways to wake up in the
morning than with a soggy pillow. If you've reached your
early sixties and that's the only thing you've got to complain about, I think you're doing pretty well, to be honest.
As for a cure, try blow-drying the inside of your mouth
before going to bed. Or put a raincoat over your pillow
case.

E.

Ears (Ringing in)

Dear Dr Ozzy:
I have two boys in a metal band and they've been
practising in my home for the past four years. Now I
have ringing in my ears. Any advice?
Grace, Miami

A classic case of *heavy metal-itus*. I suffer from permanent
tinnitus because of all the headbanging I've done over the
years, which means I've now got this constant ringing in
my ears, like a 'WEEEE' noise, but louder. It's also made
me somewhat deaf (or 'conveniently deaf', as Sharon calls
it). The sad thing is that there's an easy way to prevent tinnitus – buying a pair of ear-plugs. Do it now, before the
damage gets any worse.

Eyelids (Quivering)

Dear Dr Ozzy:
When I'm very tired, my eyelids quiver. It's quite embarrassing – is there a way of stopping it?
Lucy, New York

You've gotta listen to your body, man. If you stayed up all night and ended up with a headache and an upset stomach, you wouldn't think twice about what to do: *you'd go to bed.* But a lot of people who get only five or six hours of kip every night can't understand why they need half a gallon of espresso just to get out of bed in the morning. Clearly, in your case, your body is screaming at you that it wants more rest. I'm exactly the same way: I might be the Prince of Darkness, but if I don't get my afternoon nap, I'm useless for the rest of the day. That's why Europeans invented the siesta.

F.

Farts (Storage of)

Dear Dr Ozzy:
A new book claims that during the Great Plague of London in 1665, people were told to store their farts in a jar and sniff them if they felt unwell. Have you ever attempted to do this? How would one go about storing an outbreak of gas in an enclosed space?
Ellen, Beijing

It always blows my mind, the things people used to do to themselves before modern medicine. Could you imagine sitting on the sofa with a cup of tea and the newspaper, saying, 'Darling, pass the jam jar, I've got a bit of a headache'? Then again, they didn't have aspirin, so what were they supposed to do? And, no, I've never tried this myself – I might be crazy, but I ain't *that* crazy. When an ill wind blows in my house, I'm more worried about opening the windows before Sharon gets home than trying to save it for later.

Flies & Other Insects (Swallowed)

Dear Dr Ozzy:
I recently swallowed a fly while horse riding. Now I'm in a panic: will it give me an awful disease?
Nicola, East Finchley

I know how you feel: I was riding a motorcycle once with the visor up, and a bumble bee went down my throat. Not that it felt like a bumble bee, mind you – at the speed I was going, I thought I'd swallowed a fucking pigeon. People think that eating a bat is bad, but, believe me, inhaling a bee at 70 m.p.h. is even worse. The next day my uvula swelled up to three times its normal size and I had to have an injection. Now, that wouldn't happen with a fly. But the big problem with a fly is that you know it hasn't being doing anything pleasant lately: it certainly ain't been down the local spa, drinking honeysuckle tea. Flies eat turdburgers and bathe in their own throw-up. But don't freak out too much. Remember, cats eat flies all the time, and it never seems to do *them* any harm. So give it a few days, and if you feel okay, you're probably in the clear.

G.

Germs (in Public Loos)

Dear Dr Ozzy:
What's the point of washing your hands in a public loo if you have to open the door on the way out using a handle that's been touched by hundreds or thousands of other people who didn't wash their hands? I've tried getting around the problem by pulling my sleeve over my hand when I touch the door, but that's disgusting, too.
Chris, Newcastle

At last – someone else who gets as freaked out about this as I do. I can't fucking stand it: there you are, scrubbing your hands at the sink, but then to get out of the bog you have to grab a handle that the guy in front of you, who didn't bother to scrub-up, has just used. Let's face it, the average doorknob in a public toilet has seen more dick than a Turkish knocking shop. Like you, I've also tried using my sleeve – but all you're doing then is putting the germs on your shirt. I get so wound up about it, I've been known to rip the entire roll of paper towel off the wall and use that. *But you shouldn't have to* – they should make the doors in public toilets swing *out*, so you can open them with your foot. It ain't fucking rocket science. That way, you go in there, wash your hands, do your business, wash your hands again, then you're on your way, germ-free. If I were Prime Minister, this would be my first law.

Dear Dr Ozzy:
Regarding unhygienic door handles: I've come up with a design (patent pending) for a new kind of germ-free knob. When squeezed, it releases a dab of antiseptic liquid into your palm. Might this solve the problem?*
Tranquility, Oxford

As long as you don't end up with a hand like a snail's arse for the rest of the day, then yes. (Maybe the antiseptic stuff could be a spirit, so it evaporates?)

DR OZZY'S SURGERY NOTICEBOARD

The Trouble With Dirty Knobs

➕ Judging by the number of e-mails I keep getting about germ-covered door handles, I'm not the only one who has a serious bee up my arse on this issue. James in Aberdeen says the solution is 'mind-numbingly obvious: automatic doors. They should be law'. (I agree 1,000 per cent.) Meanwhile, Mike in Glasgow says doors aren't even necessary: 'You just need an L-shaped entrance, so passing perverts can't peek.' Pete in Merseyside has more practical advice: 'Always use your pinkie to open lav doors: you're unlikely ever to put your smallest finger in your mouth.' (Unless your name happens to be Dr Evil, Pete.) Alternatively, Marion from Aberystwyth says the trick is to 'grab a few sheets of toilet roll to protect your hands when

---

* See diagram on page 113.

opening the door, then dispose of them when you're done'. She also suggests: 'Disposable gloves should be provided in vending machines as you enter the bathroom.' Special thanks go to Gill in Cornwall, who did a Miss Marple and counted every single bloke who entered and exited the public bog at Cartgate picnic area in Somerset over the course of a weekend, then e-mailed me the results (it was a long e-mail). 'Judging by the length of time they took inside, none of them washed and dried their hands – because using the apparatus to do that takes about five minutes!' she concluded. This is the reason why people like me, who actually use the sink, get so pissed off: *what's the point of washing and drying if you've then got to touch something that's got the germs of a thousand dicks on it?* Finally, John from Bristol got in touch to suggest (as I've done myself) that building regulations need to be rewritten, making it law that public toilet doors are hung the other way around. Then our feet could do all the dirty work. David Cameron, are you listening?

HELPFUL DIAGRAM: HYGIENIC DOOR HANDLE

(The) — HANDLE-WITH CARE.

Fig. 1

APERTURES TO RELEASE ANTI-BACTERIAL substance.
Handle Entrance.
OVER COAT.

← GERMS

FLEXIBLE ELASTICATED SPONGE MATERIAL Holding Anti-Bacterial Fluid.

GERMS → Handle Entry point.

Fig. 2

Fig. 3

HANDLE ENTRANCE

GERMS ←

CISTERN. OR DOOR HANDLE.

GERMS When fitted over handle
|
FLEXIBLE
|
SPONGE.
|
FLUID CARRIER
|
ANTI-BACTERIAL.
GERMS.

Dear Dr Ozzy:
What do you make of this craze for using hand-sanitisers obsessively throughout the day? I mention it because I had to shake someone's hand at the beginning of a business meeting recently and they hadn't got rid of all the lotion, so I was left with a sticky palm. I found the whole thing quite offensive.
Eamon, Limerick

Funnily enough, a similar thing happened to me the other day with Joan Collins in the lift of my apartment building in Los Angeles. I went to shake her hand, and she said, 'Oh no, Ozzy, I can't get sick.' Mind you, I can understand the worry: I'm a singer, so if I get a cold on the road, shows can get cancelled and livelihoods are at stake. That's why I use cleanser myself every so often when I'm doing a promo. Having said that, I've never given anyone a slimer, and if anyone gave one to me, they wouldn't forget about it in a hurry. I mean, how do you even know it was *lotion* on the guy's hand? He might have just knocked one out under his desk. Personally, I would have said to him, 'What the fuck is *this*?' before wiping it on his tie.

Gilberts (Proper Disposal of)

Dear Dr Ozzy:
When I clear my throat, is it ever okay to spit? I hate swallowing, even though I know it's harmless.
Glenn, Birmingham

Depends. If you're a professional footballer, it would be rude not to. On the other hand, if you're in the middle of a business lunch, and everyone's drinking tea and eating finger sandwiches, then, no, it ain't a very good idea to start coughing up a massive Gilbert.

Golf Balls (Death by)

Dear Dr Ozzy:
My husband wants to buy a holiday home in a 'gated community' on a golf course, but I'm afraid of being killed by a stray ball. He says I'm being paranoid. Am I?
Liz, Surrey

No, you're not. When I lived in Palm Springs, Gerald Ford used to hit someone with a golf ball just about every other week. He might have hit *me*, for all I know: I was drinking so much, I wouldn't have noticed anything smaller than a flying sledgehammer. It became a standing joke after a while: you weren't a real local until you had a signed letter from the ex-president, apologising for the bump on your forehead. Not that golf balls are harmless – they're as hard as rocks and travel at over 100 m.p.h. – so, yeah, they can kill you if you're unlucky. But you have to be *very* unlucky.

H.

Hair (Self-Removal of)

Dear Dr Ozzy:
For over a year, I've been literally tearing out my hair. It started at a time when I was under immense stress, but

I haven't stopped. I'm aware that it can be described as
a mental condition – trichotillomania – but I think of it
more as an addiction. As someone who's defeated his
own vices, your wisdom would be greatly appreciated.
Eric, York

No one's ever fucking happy, are they? Half the time I'm
answering questions from blokes who'd swap their right arm
for a few more follicles. Now here you are, ripping them all
out of your own free will. Seriously, though, you should
really talk to someone about this – a shrink or at the very
least your GP – a.s.a.p. I mean, yeah, you can call it a habit,
or an addiction, or whatever, but the bottom line is that
you're harming yourself, and that's heavy duty. I wouldn't be
surprised if the rug-tugging was a symptom of some other
issues you've got going on, and if you get some treatment
now, you'll probably save yourself a lot of trouble and
heartache later. One thing you could ask your doc about is
a course of 'habit reversal training'. From what I understand,
it doesn't involve any medication, but it can be very effective.

Headbanging (Complications of)

Dear Dr Ozzy:
Your column has inspired me to go through my old
Black Sabbath collection, but now I have severe
bruising on my forehead and an intense ringing in my
ears. What's wrong with me?
Simon, Perth, Australia

It's called being a headbanger, Simon. When working-class
guys first started doing it in the early 1970s, they had never

had a way of expressing themselves before, and some of them got carried away. One guy headbanged all night at a Motörhead concert with his head *literally* inside a speaker cabinet and suffered a fatal brain haemorrhage. The thing to realise is that headbanging is just like any other exercise: the first time you do it, you're really sore the next day. You've just got to start slowly and keep it up, gradually working your way up to full match fitness. So next time, before putting on your Black Sabbath records, try doing twenty headbangs every morning for a few weeks in advance. That should help.

Dear Dr Ozzy:
I'm nineteen years old and have rheumatoid arthritis and ankylosing spondylitis (the same back disease that Mick Mars from Mötley Crüe has). I love headbanging, but can barely move when the adrenaline wears off. Any tips for muscle pain relief?
Karl, USA

I really hate to say this, but why don't you hold back on the headbanging for a bit? I know Mick, and I know how painful that condition can be. You've got to accommodate what your body can do. People can enjoy music in all kinds of different ways. What amazes me is that I often get deaf people coming to my gigs: they can't hear the lyrics, but they can get into the rhythm. So my advice is to keep going to the shows, but get into the vibe in a way that doesn't involve the mosh pit. It ain't worth the agony, man. And I certainly wouldn't recommend popping any heavy-duty pain pills – unless your doctor says you should – as they can be horrendously addictive.

Head Cold (Flying with)

Dear Dr Ozzy:
The other day I flew to a conference with a 'head cold',
thinking the change in pressure might clear out my ears.
Instead it felt as though my brain was about to explode,
and when we finally landed – after what seemed like
years – I was deaf on one side (I still am). Help!
Lisa, Reading

This ain't much use to you now, Lisa, but you should *never* fly with a really bad head cold, 'cos you can burst your eardrums. So, in future, do the opposite of what you did. Rent a car, take a boat – swim, if you have to. *But don't get on a plane.* I've heard that you can also buy these plug things that help regulate the pressure. But you've gotta use them properly, and, personally, I have trouble getting my telly to work, never mind trying to put some microscopic shield in my ear. In the meantime, you need to get checked out by a doc, 'cos you might have done yourself some damage. It's too important to wait and see if it heals by itself.

Hernia (Lump Caused by)

Dear Dr Ozzy:
I have a hiatus hernia which I've been treating for a few
years with Gaviscon tablets, without much
improvement. What really bothers me, however, is the
lump – a small, circular ball on my navel. Any ideas on
how to get rid of this unsightly bulge?
'Mike', Harrow

A friend of mine had the same thing, and unfortunately you can't just tap it a couple of times with a hammer to pop it back in – you need surgery. But this is something you *have* to get checked out by your doc, 'cos it might be more (or less) complicated than you think.

I.

Insect Bites

Dear Dr Ozzy:
On Tuesday I was cutting bushes in my yard when I accidentally made contact with a bee's nest and was attacked. I only got stung once before I dove into my pool. Two days later, my leg is twice the size it once was. What's wrong with me?
Chris, Danvers, Massachusetts

I once had a keyboard player who had to call for an ambulance if he got stung by a bee. Some people are just a lot more allergic to stings than others, and it sounds like you're having a very nasty reaction. Get it seen to immediately. Hop to the ER if necessary.

J.

Jimmy Legs (a.k.a. Restless Legs)

Dear Dr Ozzy:
I suffer from 'Jimmy legs', also known as restless leg syndrome. My legs shake and move about in the night,

**and it's driving my wife mad. Any ideas how I can put a
stop to this?**
Mick, West Midlands

I have exactly the same problem – and so does my wife.
We're like a pair of pneumatic drills, jiggling and wobbling
away under the sheets, making the floorboards rattle. My
leg has a mind of its own. It goes all over the place. Even
when I'm sitting down on the sofa, it's bouncing around
like I'm in the back of a rickshaw on a bumpy road. It's one
of the reasons why I can't stay still for more than a few minutes. In terms of treatment, you can get medication for
Jimmy legs, but it's a form of benzodiazepine – the same
thing as Valium. I spent decades trying to get off that shit,
and I don't want to go back on it. Maybe it's something
you could try, though, if you don't have a history with that
drug. Personally, I've decided just to live with the condition. I mean, it's not like it's painful. It's just irritating . . .
and wears out the bed springs pretty quick.

DR OZZY'S SURGERY NOTICEBOARD

The Battle of Bouncing Knee

➕ I always crap myself when a real doctor writes to me,
'cos I think I'm about to get a bollocking. Most of the
time, though, they just have a helpful suggestion. For
example, Dr Geoff, a retired GP from St Ives, sent me an
e-mail to say 'small doses of anti-Parkinsonian drugs
such as Pramipexole [Mirapexin]' can help cure your
restless legs. (Of course, you should *always* talk to your

own GP before trying *any* kind of treatment.) Other readers have said that mineral salts, magnesium, Crampex
tablets, and even putting a tablet of toilet soap under the
bed sheets can do some good. They also say you should
avoid peppermint mouthwash and raspberries. How
anyone could prove that is beyond me, though.

Dear Dr Ozzy:
Thanks to a suggestion by one of your readers the other
week, I've been prescribed an anti-Parkinsonian drug
for my restless leg syndrome. But when I looked online,
I found that the side-effects might include 'intense
urges to gamble' and 'increased sexual urges
(hypersexuality)'. Should I throw the pills in the bin?
David, Buckinghamshire

And you're *worried* about this? The label might as well say,
'Side-effects include having a good time.' In all seriousness,
though, there's no point curing your restless legs only to
blow your life savings in Las Vegas on blackjack and hook-
ers. Talk to your GP about your concerns.

K.

King's Speech Technique (Stuttering)

Dear Dr Ozzy:
As a self-confessed stutterer, have you ever gone
through any of the treatments shown in the film *The*

King' Speech, like putting marbles in your mouth or
reciting Shakespeare while wearing headphones? Do
you think a stutter can be cured?
Kim, Santa Barbara

I don't know if a stutter can be cured, but I can tell you
how to get one – drink and do drugs for forty years.
Believe me, getting to the end of a single sentence is a
major achievement when you're on your second bottle of
cognac and third speedball before breakfast. To answer the
first part of your question, though: no, I've never had
speech therapy . . . although I was once hypnotised by Paul
McKenna when I was trying to change my lifestyle. The
trouble was I was blasted at the time, so it's hard to say if I
was hypnotised or if I just passed out, which was a daily
occurrence in those days. As for my stutter, it's been a lot
better since I sobered up, and I've realised that it's usually
brought on by anxiety. When I'm nervous about something, my mind spins faster than my mouth can catch up,
so I end up sounding like a Second World War machine-
gun. By taking a deep breath and slowing down a bit, I can
usually keep it under control.

L.

Lead (Poisoning)

Dear Dr Ozzy:
I'm currently renovating my family's Georgian
townhouse and have just come across a government
leaflet about lead paint. Now I'm terrified that every

little thing I do will create poisonous dust that will brain-damage my toddler and pregnant wife. Please help.
Ryan, Edinburgh

A lot of people might not take this kind of thing very seriously, but I had a cousin who was an industrial painter, and he got asbestosis. So, if I were you, I'd be wearing a rubber suit and a gas mask in the house. Okay, people my age used to chew on toy soldiers made of lead ... after painting them with lead paint and licking the fucking brushes, but that doesn't make it any less dangerous. Kids also used to ride in cars without seat belts while their parents smoked themselves blue in the face with the windows closed – and we don't do *that* now. Call your local council, ask them what the right procedure is, and follow it to the letter. Meanwhile, if you've already started to sand the woodwork, send your wife and toddler to the in-laws until the job's all done and you've been given the all clear by a qualified inspector.

DR OZZY'S SURGERY NOTICEBOARD

Heavy Metal Madness

➕ Tristan Olivier from the Lead Paint Safety Association (LiPSA) tells me that local councils might not be much help when it comes to advice on handling toxic dust in old houses (see Ryan from Edinburgh, above). 'Given the extent to which childhood lead exposure is linked to reduced IQ, learning and behaviour problems, this is probably the biggest, least-known and worst-addressed public health issue in the UK,' he says. For more info, visit the LiPSA's website, at www.lipsa.org.uk.

Legs (Sleepy)

Dear Dr Ozzy:
My leg keeps 'falling asleep' without any warning. Does this mean I have poor circulation?
Lauren, Sheffield

One time, I got drunk – *badly* drunk, on cognac – and went to sleep in the wrong position. When I woke up, the lower half of my leg felt like it wasn't even there any more. It was just this useless lump attached to my thigh. At first I didn't think it was a problem . . . but it went on for *three months.* I went to my doc, and he told me – *seriously* – that he might have to chop it off. I said, 'I'm a rock'n'roll star! I can't hobble around the stage with a wooden leg, singing "Iron Man"!' Eventually, another doctor took a look at it and said it was probably caused by my alcoholism. So, if you're a heavy drinker, I'd recommend cutting down . . . or giving up entirely. Otherwise, make sure you don't sit in the same position for a long time. And if you go and see a doctor, remember, if he ever starts using phrases like 'electric saw' and 'operating table', there's nothing stopping you from getting a second opinion. I'm certainly fucking glad I did!

M.

Mourning

Dear Dr Ozzy:
My wife died in January. I've been having counselling
for the last six months but it's very lonely with just me
and my two Bedlington terriers. I feel as though I have
so much free time and need to fill it. Can you offer any
advice on coping with grief?
David, London

The thing I realised when I lost someone who was very close to me – my guitarist Randy Rhoads – is that no one can ever really prepare you for coping with sudden death. You're pretty much on your own. What you've got to come to terms with is that grief is simply a natural process, and that everyone goes through it at some point in their life. The best thing you can do is join a counselling group, or at least find *someone* to talk to about it – which it sounds like you're doing already. Having said that, of course, I didn't take any of that advice when Randy died. I locked the grief away, so it manifested itself in other ways, like drugs and alcohol. The trouble was, when I was kid, we all thought that anyone who went to therapy was one step away from the funny farm. I know better now. I suppose another thing you've gotta accept is that you never *fully* get over the death of someone who's been that close to you. I mean, even today, when I'm on stage playing any of the songs from my two albums with Randy, it's as though he's right there at my side. But it's a good feeling now, not a bad one.

Dear Dr Ozzy:
I keep suffering terrible anxiety attacks. It started when
my uncle – who was like a dad to me – died in his sleep
from a random cardiac arrest (I never met my real dad
until I was thirteen). I've been to psychologists, but all they
tell me is that if I realise I'm not going to die, the panic will
go away. That's bullshit, because I know I won't die . . . but
I still feel like I'm about to blow up inside. Please help.
Don (seventeen years old), Texas

Sounds like grief to me, Don. People don't take grief seriously enough, because the loss of someone, or even
some*thing*, can be very hard to get over. It sounds crazy, but
when I was in rehab, I had to attend 'grief groups' for the
loss of drugs and alcohol in my life. I thought it was stupid
at first – especially when I met a guy in there who was sob-
bing about his recently departed cat – but I soon discovered
that grief can mess you up badly. I wouldn't be surprised if
that's what's causing your panic attacks. Your body is over-
loaded with emotion. So my recommendation would be
that you get on the internet and find your own local grief
group. It's a lot healthier than going to your GP for a bottle
of Valium: that'll just fix one problem and start five others.

N.

Napping (Guidelines Regarding)

Dear Dr Ozzy:
What's the ideal length for an afternoon nap? My
friends swear by them, but every time I doze off during

the day I wake up in a terrible mood with a splitting
headache.
Ross, Aberdeen

I never used to understand naps. When I was a kid, I'd see
my old man dozing off in his favourite chair and think: You
went to bed last night. Why d'you need to sleep *now* as
well? But as I got older myself, I began to understand. For
me, the point of a nap isn't about sleep: it's just about getting some 'quiet time', so you can recharge. It's a break
from all the craziness of modern life. So if you find you
always wake up from a nap feeling like a dog's arsehole, just
try giving yourself twenty or thirty chilled-out minutes on
your own instead. Read, do some stretching exercises, or
go for a walk.

Nightmares (Prevention of)

Dear Dr Ozzy:
What can I do before I go to bed to prevent bad
dreams?
William, Alnwick

Personally, I've never had a problem with nightmares.
Every so often I'll have a really *confusing* dream. But I've
never had to face a zombie Esther Rantzen shooting
blood from her eyeballs and trying to cut out my liver
with a BBC letter-opener. Mind you, I didn't dream *at all*
for about forty years, because I never went to bed. The
only rest I got was when I blacked out every three or four
days. One time, when I was on tour in America with
Mötley Crüe, I passed out in the central reservation of a

twelve-lane freeway (I'd been looking for somewhere to take a piss). Back then, *waking up* was always the biggest nightmare for me. But I wouldn't recommend my former lifestyle as a way to avoid bad dreams. Instead, try thinking about something that makes you feel really good before you shut your eyes. Or have a nice cup of tea. Try camomile, if builder's brew winds you up too much. Whatever you do, avoid sleeping pills at all costs, or you might end up with a worse problem than the one you started with.

Night Sweats

Dear Dr Ozzy:
Almost every night I wake up in the early hours drenched in sweat. It's disgusting – the sheets are soaked through. I've tried to turn up the air conditioning, but to no effect. What's causing this, and how do I stop it from happening?
Olivia, New York

Could be nylon sheets. Those things make me sweat like I'm on Death Row. I can't have 'em near me. Same with feather pillows, which mess up my chest, and sleeping bags, which are one step removed from being buried alive. If it ain't your sheets, it could be what you're wearing in bed, or an allergy, or a side-effect of some medication you're taking. If I were you, I'd try something different every night, and try to solve it that way.

DR OZZY'S SURGERY NOTICEBOARD

Wet Dreams

✚ It's amazing how many people wake up in the morning feeling sweatier than one of Jabba the Hutt's armpits. One reader, Lisa, wrote: 'I suffered night sweats for fifteen years before a gynaecologist did a blood test and diagnosed that I had next to no oestrogen. Although I wasn't menopausal or pre-menopausal, I was having the same kind of symptoms. Now I take a daily supplement and my life has changed utterly.' Meanwhile, Gabrielle from London reckoned she solved the problem with a silk-filled duvet. And an anonymous GP from Scotland said a bad case of the sweats might be a symptom of something called 'polymyalgia rheumatica'. I'm told that means 'pain in many muscles' in Greek. Sounds like one of my mid-1980s hangovers.

Nipples (Unusual)

Dear Dr Ozzy:
Like Francisco Scaramanga in *The Man with the Golden Gun*, I have a third nipple. Should I be worried?
Gary, Dorset

Only if it starts talking to you.

O.

Obscene Language (Excessive Use of)

Dear Dr Ozzy:
I've become addicted to swearing. It started two years ago, and I swear in nearly every sentence now, even in front of my parents and at school. I've tried to stop but can't. I think I must have Tourette's syndrome. What should I do?
Ben, Cheshire

Swear words are weird, aren't they? I mean, the American word 'schmuck' – which pretty much no one finds offensive – apparently comes from the Yiddish word '*shmok*', which is a *very* rude term for a bloke's upstanding citizen. It's considered as bad as calling someone the C-word. Then there's one of my favourite words – 'bollocks' – which used to be slang for a vicar, or so I've been told (although in the old days a more common way of spelling it was 'ballocks'). People just decide which words they want to get upset about, basically. So my advice to you, Ben, is to carry on swearing as much as you like, but do it in a foreign language. That way, you won't get into any trouble.

P.

Pain (Management of)

Dear Dr Ozzy:
A few weeks ago, while in a New York hotel room, I
accidentally stepped on the door stop. The pain was
intense. Now, three weeks later, it hurts when I walk. I
think I might have broken something in my foot. What's
your expert medical opinion?
Mark, Rancho Santa Fe

There's an easy way to find out, Mark: trying playing football. You'll soon know if it's broken.

Dear Dr Ozzy:
I have just had a gallbladder operation and, frankly, I
feel bloody awful. Given the many medical disasters
you've recovered from during your lifetime, what are
your rehabilitation tips?
Hec, Glasgow

Two words: baby steps. You've just had someone rip open your abdomen with a knife, so you can't expect to be starring in *Riverdance* any time soon. Having said that, I wasn't very patient after I fell off my quad bike and ended up in a coma for eight days. As soon as I woke up, I tried to check myself out. Hospitals aren't very nice places to be, in my opinion – if only because there's fuck all to do in them. But I've now learned that you've gotta go easy on yourself as much as you can. Trust me, if you're impatient, you'll slow down your recovery in the long term.

Parents (Living With)

Dear Dr Ozzy:
Okay, I'm just going to come out and say it: I'm forty years old, between jobs, and single. How bad is it if I move back in with my parents, who have plenty of room at home? I'm not relishing the thought, but it would save money while I get my life together.
Robert, Pontefract

It sounds like you're trying to live your life by other people's rules. If you like your parents, and they don't mind you in their house, then move in. If you were Italian, you wouldn't even think twice about it – most guys over there live with their mothers until they get hitched, no matter how long it takes. I realise people might not be so cool with that kind of thing in West Yorkshire, but it's a lot fucking better than being so broke you can't afford to eat, never mind pay for dates. Just do what you've gotta do, man.

Phobias (Pigeons, etc.)

Dear Dr Ozzy:
Every time I get on a plane, I convince myself that I'm going to die. It's reached the point where I'm starting to make excuses at work to avoid travelling overseas.
Please help!
Liz, Buckinghamshire

Flying *can* be deadly. For example, I was once on a plane to America and the bloke next to me started to make funny noises while eating his complementary peanuts. Next thing I knew, I was sitting next to a corpse. The worst thing was having to press the little buzzer to call for a flight attendant, and then explaining why a bloke who'd been alive a few minutes earlier was suddenly face down on his tray table. For a moment, I thought they'd send out Columbo to meet me when I landed at JFK. In the end, they put a blanket over him, moved me to a seat in first class, and kept the champagne coming. I mention this story only because I'm told that having someone drop dead next to you is more likely than your plane falling out of the sky. You're also more likely to die in a car crash on the way to the airport than in a plane crash. But not many people lie awake at night worrying about the drive to Heathrow. Try reminding yourself of that next time you have to fly somewhere. It might calm you down.

Dear Dr Ozzy:
My friend has a rare phobia: she's terrified of pigeons.
Is there a cure?
Anna, Finland

I ain't got a clue, but if your friend lives in Finland too, how many pigeons does she come across on a daily basis? I mean, if she lived in the middle of Trafalgar Square, it might be problem. As it is, just be glad she's not freaked out by reindeer.

Dear Dr Ozzy:
I'm terrified of butterflies. Is this is a common phobia?
And what should I do now that summer is approaching

and my room will soon become infested with the
horrible things?
Lola, Irish Republic

I had no idea it was possible to get so upset about butterflies.
I mean, what else scares you? Rainbows, puppies, sunny
days? Personally, the only creatures I really can't stand are
rats. If I see one, I freak, big time. But what can you do?
You can't walk around all day in a hazmat suit with a bag
over your head on the off-chance you might come across
one. Having said that, it's pretty easy to stay out of the way
of rats, but it might be a bit harder with butterflies. If it's
causing you a lot of anxiety, talk to your GP. Maybe he'll be
able to sign you up for some kind of desensitization therapy.

Q.

Quinquaud's Decalvans Folliculitis*

R.

Rabies (Suspected)

Dear Dr Ozzy:
How can I tell if I've got rabies? The reason I ask is
because I was bitten by a stray dog while on holiday in

---

* I'm fucked if I know what this is, but it was all I could find that began with the
letter 'Q'.

Turkey, and now I'm worried it might have given me a
terrible disease.
Denise, Portsmouth

I thought I'd caught rabies after eating that bat in Des
Moines, Iowa. The injections they gave me were horrendous: one in each arm, one in each arse cheek, one in
each thigh. Then you've got to rub the stuff like crazy to
make it spread over the muscle. It's like an oil, very
dense – you can feel it trickling around inside you. It's the
safest thing to do, and I'm sure the treatment has improved
since 1982, but it ain't very nice. Personally, I gave up
halfway through. I said to Sharon, 'If I start barking, we
can start up again.'

DR OZZY'S SURGERY NOTICEBOARD

Going Batty

➕ According to Bernard in London, anyone who gets
bitten by a stray animal in a distant country should go
and see a doctor immediately – not wait until they start
howling at the moon – 'cos it could be 'a life and death
matter'. Even though I didn't finish my own rabies
treatment in 1982 after eating a bat's head on stage,
Bernard says the injections I had in hospital later that
night may well have saved my life.

S.

Sleeping Pills

Dear Dr Ozzy:
I can't stop taking sleeping pills. This has been going on for about five years now. I'm out of work and at a loss what to do. Help.
Yoshizawa, Japan

I'm convinced that once you start relying on sleeping pills, it damages your sleeping pattern for ever. A lot of sleeping pills are made from benzodiazepine – the same drugs family as Valium and very addictive stuff. When I finally got off it after twenty-five years, it was the worst withdrawal I ever had. The way I stopped was by switching my sleeping medication to an anti-depressant called trazodone. It worked for me, so I recommend that you talk to your doctor about doing something similar. The secret is to go very slowly: there's no hurry. I also tried using a non-benzodiazepine sleeping pill, Ambien – also known as zolpidem – but it was the worst. My short-term memory got so bad I didn't even know what time of day it was. Mind you, I was popping the fucking things like M&Ms.

Sleepwalking

Dear Dr Ozzy:
I keep waking up in my next-door neighbour's front garden. I live alone, so either someone is coming into

my house in the middle of the night and carrying me
there or I'm sleepwalking. What can I do about it?
Jane, Bradford

I'm always pottering about in the middle of the night,
fast asleep. I was in a B&B one time, and I sleepwalked
into the wrong room, got into bed, and carried on with
whatever dream I was having. Then this big hairy bloke
climbed between the sheets with me. I woke up and said,
'What are you doing here?' He took one look at me,
screamed, clapped his hands over his wedding tackle,
and shouted back, 'WHAT THE FUCK ARE *YOU*
DOING HERE?' Sadly, there ain't no cure for sleepwalking, as far as I know. But it's not always a bad thing.
A few years ago, for example, I was sleepwalking around
my house in Buckinghamshire, when I walked smack
into a burglar. If that doesn't wake you up, nothing will.
I almost caught the guy, too. I put him in a headlock for
about five minutes, but I didn't have any handcuffs or
anything, so in the end I just threw him out of the
window. He hobbled off across the field with about two
million quid's worth of Sharon's jewellery in a carrier
bag. Still, looking on the bright side, if I hadn't been
sleepwalking, I never would have got to meet a genuine
diamond thief.

Snoring

Dear Dr Ozzy:
Is a marriage automatically dead if the two parties start
using separate bedrooms? I ask because my wife has
developed a snore that's loud enough to wake the

mummies in Egypt, and I can't sleep next to her without
large and unwise doses of medication.
Viv, Hull

Relax, your marriage ain't over. I know quite a few people
with very healthy relationships who sleep in different rooms
'cos they don't want to listen to a human chainsaw next to
them when they're trying to get some shut-eye. I mean, if
you're the first one to drop off, it ain't a problem, but for
the poor sod who's still awake, it's excruciating. Having said
all that, you might want to look into some anti-snoring
gizmos before choosing the separate-bedroom option. The
internet has all kinds of things, from mouthpieces to nostril expanders to special pillows. Why not give some of 'em
a try?

T.

Transvestism

Dear Dr Ozzy:
For years, I've fantasised about what it would be like to
be a woman – to the extent where I've started to shop
for girls' clothing and wear my wife's underwear when
she's away on business. How can I explain this to her?
Or is that a terrible idea?
David, Watford

Okay, you've got two choices, David: pluck up the
courage to tell her now; or get caught later. It's really that
simple. As much as you think you can hide this for ever,

it's obviously such a big part of who you are that I guarantee one day you'll have a couple of drinks, put on a frock, and the missus will come home early and hit the roof. That's gonna be a much harder conversation than if you bring it up gently at your own pace. And you never know, your wife might not even care. I mean, here in Los Angeles, there's even a society for cross-dressers. They're all builders, postmen, delivery boys or whatever. They get dressed up in their fishnets for a night of clubbing, then go to work the next day in their overalls as if nothing had happened.

Tubs (Hot)

Dear Dr Ozzy:
My husband has bought a 'hot tub' and put it in our back garden, but I refuse to get in it, because I've heard horror stories about the water becoming a breeding-ground for germs. He says I'm worrying too much, and now spends half the weekend in there. What's your opinion?
Betty, Portsmouth

You're *both* right. There's nothing better than being outdoors in a hot tub on a crisp October evening, drinking a nice glass of something cold. But if you don't maintain a hot tub properly, it can turn into a swamp, with algae and frogs and fuck knows what else floating around in there. I mean, even though it's all sleek and shiny, with pressure jets and mood lighting, a hot tub is still basically just a big bubbling cauldron of chemicals. It's worst when you have a party and a bunch of hairy blokes climb in there, all burping and farting and blowing their noses. That grosses me out. Another thing with hot tubs: you've gotta watch the heat. I used to get blasted on cocaine, feel my heart begin to pound, then try to calm down by jumping into 900-degree water. One time, I swear my head almost *exploded*. But if your husband gets his new toy cleaned regularly – tell him to sign up for a weekly maintenance service – there's no reason not to take a dip. You never know, it might even improve your love life.

U.

Urination (Nervous Pisser Syndrome)

Dear Dr Ozzy:
If I'm standing next to another man at a public urinal, I can't pee. Even if I'm desperate to go – not a drop. I once queued up for twenty minutes at a rock concert to use the loo and then had to walk away because I was wedged between two big blokes. I've never known any of my friends to have the same problem. What's wrong with me?
Terry, Essex

Let me ask you a question, Terry: when this happens, are you *absolutely sure* you need to pee? When I need to relieve myself, there ain't no choice about it. I don't care if the Coldstream Guards are standing next to me – whatever's inside is coming out. So my advice is to wait until you're desperate to go. Or see a shrink: it might be anxiety.

DR OZZY'S SURGERY NOTICEBOARD

'Performance' Anxiety

✚ Important news from Ray in Suffolk: 'According to a study of public urinal usage in America, "flow start" was delayed by an average of twenty seconds when two blokes were standing right next to each other – as opposed to a solo effort.' So poor old Terry obviously ain't suffering alone.

V.

Vaginas (Fishy)

Dear Dr Ozzy:
I've been told that the best way to prevent unpleasant odour in your private areas is not to use soap, only water. This sounds a bit counter-intuitive to me. Could it be true? Tyler (no address given)

It would help to know if you were a guy or a girl. Assuming you own a pair of testicles, whoever gave you this advice obviously wasn't planning on sitting next to you in a hot car any time soon. In general, avoiding soap is never gonna prevent unpleasant odours. The only thing it's gonna prevent is you making any friends – unless you're using a power hose (which I obviously don't recommend). If you're a member of the more complicated sex, on the other hand, my wife tells me that you do need to be very careful when it comes to soap and your sensitive areas, especially if you like lathering yourself up with the heavily scented grandma-type stuff. Bear in mind, though: the Prince of Darkness ain't exactly a world authority on female anatomy. If you're really concerned about it, get yourself an appointment with a gynaecologist.

Vertigo

Dear Dr Ozzy:
I suffer from vertigo. What can I do to cure it?
Nilay, Istanbul

I thought I had vertigo for forty years. I eventually went to the doctor and he said, 'Mr Osbourne, the problem – as far as I can tell – is that you're drunk. Very drunk.' So my advice to you, Nilay, is to go to bed for twenty-four hours, drink *nothing* apart from water, then get up and walk around in circles for a bit. If you're still feeling dizzy, you might have a genuine problem.

W.

Wax (Big Lumps of)

Dear Dr Ozzy:
I used a cotton-wool bud to clean out my ears the other day and dislodged some wax. Now I'm half deaf. Is there an easy way to get rid of the wax without going to the doctor?
Lucy, Carlisle

Short answer: no. Go to a doctor. I remember getting a smack around the head once from Sharon – her hand clipped the wrong spot and burst my eardrum. I had to wear a plug in my ear for ages while it healed. It was like walking around with a cardboard box on my head. Sharon felt terrible. Not as bad as I felt, though. So don't mess around with your ears: they're too important, and too easy to break.

Weird Shit

Dear Dr Ozzy:
If I open my mouth in a certain way, I can fire saliva like it's a water pistol. What should I do?
Christopher, Bristol

Don't open your mouth. That should fix it.

X.

X-Rays (Dangers of)

Dear Dr Ozzy:
Thanks to airport scanners, the new 3-D imaging equipment in my dentist's office, and cosmic radiation from long-haul flights, I'm worried that I'm turning into a one-man Chernobyl. Should I try to cut down on all of this radiation exposure?
Brad, Somerset

You're talking to someone who's been flying on a weekly basis since the late 1960s. I probably give off more cosmic radiation than Halley's fucking Comet – and that's before adding in all the airport scans I've had, or the thousands of visits to my dentist. Having said that, by far the longest exposure I ever had to an X-ray was for the cover of one of my albums, *Down to Earth*. The bloke in charge of the artwork had to shout directions to me through a four-foot-thick brick wall, 'cos he was so scared of getting cancer. At that point in my life, though, getting zapped with death rays was probably the safest thing I did all year. These days, radiation is just a fact of life, so there's no point in letting it drive you nuts. I mean, yeah, it's a pain in the arse going through airport security, but your chances of getting sick have gotta be close to zero. And what's the alternative? Getting blasted out of the sky at 37,000 feet? I'll take the X-ray, thanks.

Y.

Yawning (Side-Effects)

Dear Dr Ozzy:
Whenever I yawn, my eyes water – to the point where it looks like I'm about to cry. How can I stop this?
Lex, Surrey

Easy: stop doing things that make you yawn. Try skydiving instead?

Z.

Zoning Out (While Driving)

Dear Dr Ozzy:
When driving long distances, what's the best way to
stay awake at the wheel? I've tried keeping the window
open, but I still find my eyes glassing over and I have to
take a break.
Raj, Birmingham

I knew some roadies in the 1970s who could drive from
Land's End to John O'Groats and back ten times thanks to
the rocket powder they were putting up their noses on a
daily basis. But driving when you're high is as stupid as
driving when you're exhausted. Either way, you could end
up killing yourself – or, worse, someone else. If you want
to cover a lot of miles without stopping, get a co-driver. Or
take the train.

Dr Ozzy's Trivia Quiz:
Doctor! Doctor!

*Find the answers – and add up
your score – on page 282*

1. **Which drug was Harold 'Dr Death' Shipman addicted to?**
   a) Pethidine (known as Demerol in the US)
   b) Codeine
   c) Vicodin

2. **A woman in England recently started legal proceedings against her doctor for giving her what?**
   a) Two 'leg-buckling' orgasms within ninety seconds of each other
   b) Oral herpes
   c) A slap in the face to wake her up

3. **A dentist in North Carolina was accused of using a syringe to inject what into his patients' mouths?**
   a) LSD
   b) His own semen
   c) A home-made numbing gel made from dog's liver

4. **To advertise a new technique he'd invented, a British GP performed what surgery on himself?**

a) Tendon repair
b) Kneecap replacement
c) Vasectomy

5. **A survey of GPs in America found that 73 per cent of them had . . .**

a) Been turned on by a patient
b) Made sure that rude patients spent longer in the waiting room
c) Done things to patients that weren't necessary, just to look better in court if they were ever sued

7

Genetics Explained . . . Sort of

Before Reading, Apply Ice-Pack to Brain

When I got a call one morning from an editor at the *Sunday Times*, telling me that some scientists wanted to 'sequence my genome', I didn't know what to say. Not 'cos I was surprised – *nothing* surprises me any more when it comes to the crazy shit that happens in my life. I just didn't understand what the fuck he was on about. I thought he was talking about one of those little blokes you find down the bottom of the garden with a white beard and a pointy red hat.

'You *what*?' I said. 'A gnome?'

'No, a *ge*-nome,' laughed the guy on the phone. 'Basically, all your genes and the bits in between are mapped on a computer. The company that arranges it – and hires the scientists to analyse the results – is called Knome, Inc. It was founded by a top Harvard professor.'

To be honest, I didn't like the sound of it. I'm a rock star, not the Brain of Britain. And even if they did the test, how would I know what the results meant? The only Gene I'd ever known anything about was the one who played bass in Kiss. Still, it's not every day someone wants to unravel your DNA, so I asked if anyone else had had it done.

'Only about two hundred people, because the technology is so expensive,' said the bloke from the paper. 'The first human genome they ever sequenced was in 1990, but they didn't get the final results until more than a decade later – in 2003. It cost three billion dollars.'

'Well, that rules it out, then,' I said. 'I ain't got three billion dollars.'

'Prices have come down,' he replied. 'Besides, in your case, Knome say they can raise the cash from other people. They'll provide you with your entire genome on a USB drive the size of a Zippo lighter. Then they'll go through the results with you in person, line by line.'

I still didn't get it. Why spend the money on *me* when they could do someone like Stephen Hawking?

'Look,' said the editor, 'you've said it yourself: you're a *medical miracle.* You went on a drink and drugs bender for forty years. You broke your neck on a quad bike. You died twice in a chemically induced coma. You walked away from your tour bus without a scratch after it was hit by a plane. Your immune system was so compromised by your lifestyle that you got a false-positive HIV test. And yet here you are, alive and well and living in Buckinghamshire.'

'So this test can tell me why I'm still here?' I asked.

'It won't tell you everything. The scientists still have a lot more work to do before they understand how genes work. But it might help make sense of a lot of things. It will also be able to tell if anything in your genes is linked to, say, Alzheimer's disease. But you're in your sixties, so anything *really* scary in your DNA would probably have killed you a long time ago, along with that line of ants you once snorted with Mötley Crüe.'

'What if they find a new kind of gene? Will I get a disease named after me?'

'Possibly.'

That was enough for me. 'Okay,' I said. 'I'll do it.'

A few weeks later, a medic came to my house in Chalfont St Peter to take a blood sample. I was having a rare day off from my world tour at the time, I was knackered, and I began to wonder what the fuck I was doing. I mean, it's not a great feeling, being a human Petri dish. Then again, I was curious. Given the swimming pools of booze I've guzzled over the years – not to mention the cocaine, morphine, sleeping pills, cough syrup, LSD, Rohypnol ... you name it – there's really no plausible medical reason why I should still be alive. Maybe my DNA could provide the answer.

As soon as the guy in the white coat had taken his sample, he put the test tube in an envelope and told me he was going to send it off to a lab in New Jersey. 'First, they'll extract the DNA, then they'll process it at a place called Cofactor Genomics in St Louis, Missouri,' he said. 'At Cofactor, they use a machine that costs almost half a million quid to read your DNA and "sequence" your genes, then they'll save the whole thing on to a hard drive and post it back to Knome. After that, researchers will go through it all with a fine-tooth comb, to see what your genes have to say about you. Start to finish, the whole thing should take about thirteen weeks. Not bad, when the first one took thirteen years.'*

---

* My personal assistant, Tony, took notes during this meeting, and when I got the results from Dr Nathan a few months later. Obviously, I never would have been able to remember all of the technical stuff otherwise.

'Next year it'll probably take thirteen fucking minutes,'
I said.

The guy just smiled nervously. Then he cleared off,
sharpish.

The next day I went back to my tour and put it all out
of my mind.

It was three months later when I finally got a call saying
they were gonna send over another bloke – Dr Nathan –
with my results. Sharon couldn't be with me for the pres-
entation 'cos of some badly timed meetings in Los Angeles,
so she called him beforehand to make sure he wasn't going
to tell me that my head will explode in 2013 or some other
horrendous news. Strangely, though, I wasn't nervous.
Probably 'cos I wasn't expecting to understand a word of
what he had to say.

I've since learned that Dr Nathan – who looks way too
young to have loads of letters after his name – is an expert
in 'primate DNA'. And I have to say, I felt pretty primitive
when I was listening to him: it was like he'd swallowed
Google for breakfast, then scoffed a couple of encyclope-
dias for lunch. First, he gave me a silver box with some
Latin words on the lid. 'It means "Know Thyself",' he told
me. 'It's from the Temple of Apollo.' When I opened it up,
there was one of those little USB drives inside. The doc
took it out, popped it into his laptop, and the screen filled
up with about ten billion numbers and letters . . . line after
line after line after line of 'em. It would have taken me ten
years to read one page. 'Well, there it is,' said Dr Nathan,
proudly. 'Your genome.'

'Okay,' I said. 'But what the fuck does it all *mean*?'

'Well, it shows you pretty much all of the twenty to
twenty-five thousand genes in your body,' he explained.
'Better than that, it tells you in *what order* they're put

together. Then it cross-checks that with other people's genomes. Now, most people's genomes are very similar, because we're all the same species, right? But there are all kinds of tiny differences that let you see what traits you have, or what diseases you might get.'

The craziest thing Dr Nathan told me was that we *all* have the Huntington's gene – it's if you're *missing* any genes that you're in really big trouble – but only people with certain types will ever come down with the disease. Another thing that blew me away was how much they already know about the genes involved in diseases like Huntington's: even if you don't suffer from it yourself, your DNA can tell doctors straight away if you're likely to pass it on to your kids. That's pretty heavy-duty stuff, and I can see why a lot of people might not want to know. Personally, I'm not that bothered. I've already had all my kids, so it's too late to worry about it now. And even if my DNA told me I was a gonner, I could still get run over by a lorry tomorrow – or poisoned by a radioactive duck turd – long before whatever they found had a chance to kill me. We all have to die of something anyway. At least if you know what's coming, you might get a chance to put it off for a while.

Dr Nathan also reminded me that all of this genome stuff is still in its very early days. Until everyone on the planet has had the test done – and the results are fed into some megacomputer, along with everyone's medical records – it'll be more for scientists and rich nerds than anyone else. As the doc put it: 'Looking at someone's genome today is a bit like watching colour TV on a black-and-white set.'

But even that lets you see a picture – and Dr Nathan had some pretty far-out things to tell me. The first big piece of news was that I have a famous cousin I never knew about:

Stephen Colbert, the American funny guy. 'You both have mitochondrial DNA passed down from your mothers in Haplogroup-T,' he said.

'Haplo . . . *what?*'

'Put it this way, fewer than three per cent of people of European descent are in this group,' Dr Nathan said. 'Colbert hasn't had his full genome sequenced, but he did have that part of his DNA tested – for a second time, actually – just a few months ago, which is how we know. In the grand scheme of things, you're close cousins. Your mothers' lines go back to a pair of sisters a few thousand years ago. Our best guess is that they were living in the area of the Black Sea at the time. Most randomly chosen people would have to go back about ninety thousand years to find a common ancestor.'

There was only one problem with this life-changing revelation, as far as I was concerned. If the doc hadn't told me, I wouldn't have known who the fuck Stephen Colbert was, 'cos I'd never watched his TV show. Now, though, I'm his most loyal viewer. I mean, I'm always watching the stuff my wife does on the telly, so I should do the same for other family members. Having said that . . . why couldn't they have found out that I'm related to Paul McCartney or John Lennon? Not that I'm short of other famous cousins now, though.

'Your DNA also tested positive for an even smaller part of Haplogroup-T, called Haplogroup-T2,' said Dr Nathan.

Apparently, this means I'm a distant relation of Henry 'Skip' Gates, a big-deal Harvard professor and a mate of President Obama. (This isn't as crazy as it sounds, 'cos the guy was arrested and charged with disorderly conduct not too long ago. That's pretty good evidence of an Osbourne gene, I reckon. Or maybe not, 'cos the charges were dropped.) Other members of my extended family include Jesse and Frank James, Tsar Nicholas II and even King George I. I'm sure the royals will be over the fucking moon about that piece of information.

A lot of the other stuff in my genome was more reassuring than mind-blowing. For example, I don't have any dodgy genes that are strongly linked to cancer, Huntington's or Parkinson's. (The last bit was particularly good news, 'cos I used to be convinced I had Parkinson's disease, until my doctor diagnosed a 'Parkinsonian-like tremor'.) So maybe I'll get to live as long as my indestructible nan, who made it to the age of ninety-nine. They also found nothing in my genes to suggest I'm likely to get Alzheimer's, which was a relief, given what Sharon's dad went through with that horrendous disease.

Another thing Dr Nathan discovered was that I'm part Neanderthal. That won't come as much of a surprise to the missus . . . or various police departments around the world. But the doc thought it was pretty interesting. 'It was only a few months ago that scientists managed to sequence a Neanderthal genome from old bones found in a Croatian cave and found a link with humans,' he said. 'Previously, it was thought that all modern humans came from Africa between fifty and sixty thousand years ago. Now we know there was some Neanderthal–human interbreeding, which is why there's a small part of Neanderthal in your DNA.' This is great news for blokes everywhere, I reckon: if the Neanderthals could get lucky with human females, there's hope for us all. One thing that blew my mind was that I have *less* Neanderthal in me than quite a few very brainy people. For instance, the professor who founded Knome, George Church, has *three times* more caveman in him than I do.

Speaking of dead relatives, it also turns out that I share some DNA with the people who were killed in Pompeii when Mount Vesuvius blew its top in AD 79. (Scientists took samples from the bodies in the ash, which is how they can tell.) That means I'm probably descended from some of the survivors. Which makes a lot of sense, I suppose. If any of the Roman Osbournes drank anywhere near as much booze as I did, they wouldn't even have noticed the explosion. They probably just woke up a few days later with a splitting headache, as usual.

DR OZZY'S INSANE BUT TRUE STORIES

How the 'Osbourne Identity' Was Unlocked

- In July 2010, a 'phlebotomist' – whatever the fuck that is – took a sample of my blood and sent it to a lab in New Jersey.

- DNA was taken from my white blood cells, dissolved in a salt solution, then sent to Cofactor Genomics in St Louis.

- At Cofactor, my DNA was 'chopped up' into between ten and twenty-five trillion pieces thanks to some heavy-duty shaking. After that, they spelled out all the chemical letters – in precise order – that make me the certifiable nutter I am.

- Over the next sixteen days, Cofactor used a photo-copier-sized machine – which costs more than *three* Ferraris, I'm told – to 'read' my genome thirteen times over before saving it to a hard drive.

- The hard drive with 'me' on it was sent to Knome, Inc. in Cambridge, Massachusetts.

- Knome compared the *six billion* letters in my genome with every other genome they have on record to find out why the fuck I'm still alive. Then they put all their findings on a little USB stick and presented it to me at home.

- Finally, while trying to understand all this, my brain exploded.

Apart from the distant-ancestor stuff – which seems more fun than useful, to be honest – Dr Nathan told me some things that I thought only my wife could possibly know (although it was a struggle getting him to explain it in plain English). For example, he said, 'There are some variants in your RNASE3 gene that suggest you are two hundred and forty times more likely than other people to have allergies.' Now, the doc said you can't always trust those sorts of odds, but they happen to be spot on in my case: I'm allergic to dust mites and I get bad sinus infections. So maybe the Osbourne snot gene will help in the search for a cure for hay fever. I could think of worse ways to be remembered.

But that was just the beginning of what they found in the nose department when they were poking around in my DNA.

'You also have some non-sense variants in nine of your odour receptor genes,' said Dr Nathan.

'Eh?'

'Basically, it means you might not be able to smell a few

things. That isn't particularly unusual, because modern
humans don't have to sniff out their dinner from two miles
away, then go and club it to death. As the species has
evolved, our sense of smell has become less sensitive.'

I couldn't believe what I was hearing. My old man used
to claim that he didn't have *any* sense of smell – or very
little. We always thought he was taking the piss. Me and my
brother used to take it in turns to fart silently next to him,
just to try to catch him out. But he never responded, and
now I knew why. He was telling the truth, and it was all
because of his genes.

They also found that my body ain't any good at pro-
cessing coffee – or, as Dr Nathan put it, 'You're a slow
acetylator of caffeine because of the way your NAT2 gene
works.' That explained a lot: I like the occasional blast of
espresso, but after one shot my eyeballs feel like they're
gonna explode and I start shaking enough to register on the
Richter scale.

Dr Nathan revealed some other interesting things, too:
according to the most recent research, I'm 6.13 times more
likely than the average person to have alcohol dependency
or alcohol cravings (no argument from me there); 1.31
times more likely to have a cocaine addiction; and 2.6 times
more likely to have hallucinations while taking cannabis
(makes sense, although I was usually loaded on so many different things at the same time, it's hard to know what
caused what). Meanwhile, I scored low on the genes associated with heroin addiction: I was never addicted to street
heroin, 'cos it made me throw up – which I considered a
terrible waste of booze – although I was very addicted to
morphine for a long time. I also scored low for nicotine
addiction, which is interesting, 'cos cigarettes were the first
thing I gave up when I got sober.

To be completely honest, some the stuff Dr Nathan told me was a bit bleedin' obvious. I mean, if I'd forked out three billion dollars for the test, I wouldn't have been too impressed when he said, 'Your PTPN11 gene is normal-*ish* – so you don't have Noonan syndrome.'

'What's Noonan syndrome?' I asked.

'A type of dwarfism.'

'So, you're telling me I'm not a dwarf?'

'That's right.'

'Well, that's a relief.'

And, as I said before, they're still in the early stages of working out all this stuff. For example, Dr Nathan said I have 300,000 completely new 'spellings' in my DNA. ('Of course I do, I'm fucking dyslexic!' I told him.) But they don't really know what any of these mean. 'One of those never-seen-before things we found in your genome was a regulatory segment in your ADH4 gene, which we know metabolises alcohol,' said the doc. 'It could make you more able to break down alcohol than the average person ... or *less* able.' Given that I used to drink four bottles of cognac a day, I'm not sure anyone needs a Harvard scientist to get to the bottom of that particular mystery.

'We also found new disruptions in your TTN and CLTCL1 genes,' the doc went on. 'The first one might be associated with anything from deafness to Parkinsonianism, while we know that the second one can affect brain chemistry. If you wanted to find out more about your addictive behaviour, that might be a good place to start.'

If anything tells you how far this research still has to go, that pretty much sums it up for me. I mean, if there's a gene for addictive behaviour, you'd have thought that mine would be written in pink neon and would have a ribbon and a bow on top.

Dr Nathan was happy to discuss loads of stuff in my genome – from my Pompeii ancestors, to my snotty nose, to the fact that I'm ready to blast through the ceiling after one cup of coffee – but it was the very last thing he mentioned that really stuck in my mind. 'You have two versions of a gene known as COMT,' he said. 'The first is often called the "warrior variant" and the second is known as the "worrier variant". A lot of people have one or the other. Not many have both.'

So I suppose I'm a warrior *and* a worrier. I thought back to a time years and years ago, when I was on holiday in Hawaii with this chick I knew. We were walking along a cliff-edge one day, and she couldn't believe it when I told her I was afraid of heights. 'I'm serious,' I said. 'I'd get vertigo wearing your high heels.' She burst out laughing, and I couldn't work out what was so funny. Eventually, she said, 'You don't remember last night, do you? We were walking along this path and you ripped off your shirt and took a running jump. I don't think you even looked to see if there were any rocks below. Luckily, you hit water. Then you wanted me to jump after you.' Not being insane, she had refused.

I'd always thought it was just the booze and the drugs that made me do crazy things like that, even though I've always been a terrible hypochondriac and in some ways quite anxious and insecure. But now I was starting to think it had more to do with my genes. Being a warrior – the crazy, Alamo-pissing, bat-eating Prince of Darkness – has made me famous. Being a worrier has kept me alive when some of my dearest friends never made it beyond their mid-twenties.

Before Dr Nathan left, I told him my theory. He frowned, nodded, narrowed his eyes. Then he said, 'Look,

Mr Osbourne, after studying your history, taking your blood, extracting your genes from the white cells, making them readable, sequencing them, analysing and interpreting the data using some of the most advanced technology available in the world today – and, of course, comparing your DNA with all the current research in the US National Library of Medicine, not to mention the eighteenth revision of the public human reference genome – I think I can say with a good deal of confidence why you're still alive.'

I looked at him.

He looked at me.

'Go on, then,' I said. 'Spit it out.'

'Sharon,' he replied.

Chapter Notes:
Blame It on the DNA
(Cut Out and Keep)

	MAJOR LIFE EVENT				
	Biting head off winged nocturnal mammal	Pissing on the Alamo – by accident	Not being dead	Drinking four bottles of cognac a day during most of the 1980s	Being off my fucking rocker most of the time
Genetic cause	COMT: both variants (Val158 and Met158)	A number of genes on Chromosome 10	Haplogroup-T2	ADH4	NAT2
What it means	I'm a warrior *and* a worrier – I act like a lunatic but go to the nearest doctor the next day	Finally, it's official: I'm part-Neanderthal	Some of my distant relatives escaped from Pompeii in AD 79 (probably)	According to the doc, I have 'an unusual variant near one of my alcohol dehydro-genase genes'	My body can't process caffeine
Note to self	Did someone just call me a COMT?	Next time, say, 'Sorry, Officer, it wasn't me, it was my caveman gene!'	Survive Mount Vesuvius, and you can survive anything . . . even a bollocking from Sharon	Translation: I'm a natural-born pisshead	Drink more coffee

Dr Ozzy's Trivia Quiz:
Mutant Strains

*Find the answers – and add up
your score – on page 282*

1. **Which of these creatures might have existed many years ago – thanks to a far-out genetic mutation?**

a) Hobbits
b) Unicorns
c) Dragons

2. **What was genetically special about Lakshmi Tatama when she was born in Bihar, India, in 2005?**

a) She had four arms and four legs
b) She had a conjoined headless twin
c) She had three heads

3. **What do scientists put in genetically altered salmon to keep them alive in very cold water?**

a) Antifreeze
b) Polar bear DNA
c) Special genes that tell the fish to grow thicker skin

4. **Scientists first learned about genetics because of which garden vegetable?**

a) Carrots
b) Brussels sprouts
c) Peas

5. **The world's first cloned sheep, Dolly, was named in honour of ...**

a) One of the scientists who created her
b) Dolly Parton
c) Doncaster Polytechnic

8

Friends & Arseholes

For People who Aren't People *People*

Only two things in life are supposed to be inevitable: death and taxes. Unfortunately, that ain't true: there's something else you'll never be able to avoid, unless you live in Antarctica, Siberia or possibly Northumberland. *People.* They're everywhere. At work. In shops. On your Facebollocks website. And that's a massive problem if you ain't a 'people person', 'cos you'll end up spending half your life getting into arguments, feeling embarrassed, not knowing what to say, having the piss taken out of you, or, worst of all, just being a boring fucker at parties. Luckily, Dr Ozzy is here to help. Even if your idea of a holiday is a month by yourself in a cave, all you have to do is follow the advice in this chapter and you'll be able to handle anything another human being can throw at you. Just don't expect to like them.

Or for them to like you.

> **Dear Dr Ozzy:**
> I hate 'bear-hugging' other men, even close friends.
> How do I avoid it without offending anyone?
> Rafael, Windsor

You've got a mouth, so use it. I know some tough-guy types who think it's cool to say hello by getting me in a headlock and wrestling me to the ground – a 'buddy slam', they call it over here in California. More like a load of macho bollocks, if you ask me. If they try it now, I just tell them to fuck off. I mean, if your mates said hello by punching you in the face, you'd do something about it, right? So why not just say, 'Look, I don't like having my head in your armpit while you whack me on the back like Hulk Hogan. Can't we just shake hands or wave at each other or something?'

> **Dear Dr Ozzy:**
> I've suddenly developed a habit of putting my foot in my mouth in the most cringeworthy ways imaginable – like blurting out jokes about fat people in front of overweight friends. What could be causing this sudden outbreak of tactlessness? It's not booze, because it's happened as many times sober as it has when I'm drunk.
> Fred, Basingstoke

It won't make you feel any better, but we all drop a clanger every now and again. You can't beat yourself up about it too much, 'cos life would be pretty boring if we all talked like politicians. And believe me, your fat joke's nothing compared with the shit I used to say when I was drinking four bottles of cognac a day. For instance, I once told Brian

Wilson from the Beach Boys that I was glad his brother had just died. I phoned him the next day to apologise, and we've since become good mates, but I'm still cringing now.

> **Dear Dr Ozzy:**
> I'm a happily married man, but I keep getting inappropriate e-mails from a male co-worker. Some are just dirty jokes, but others are graphic fantasies, like how he wants to sodomize me in the disabled bathroom stall. At first it was funny, but now it's creepy and I want it to stop. Obviously, I don't want to say anything to the boss.
> Marcus, California

If someone I knew started sending me e-mails about sticking their one-eyed wonder anywhere near my rear end – as a joke or otherwise – I wouldn't be writing to Dr Ozzy for advice, I'd be telling the bloke in question to stop giving me the fucking creeps, man. How about sending this sicko a reply that says, 'Don't ever e-mail me again'? If that doesn't work, confront him in private. Or get yourself a sexual harassment lawyer.

> **Dear Dr Ozzy:**
> I recently took in a lodger, who said he was going to be staying only a fortnight – but he's still here, six months later. Worse than that, he coughs all the time. It's driving me crazy. What can I do to get rid of him, or the cough, or both? Thank you.
> Maddy, Cambridge

I've never had an annoying lodger, but I did once have a next-door neighbour who played tennis at midnight. It doesn't sound like much but, believe me, you don't want to hear *thwock, thwack, thwock* when you're trying to get some kip. It was like living on Centre Court at Wimbledon. In the end, I set up my billion-watt PA system in the garden, and the second I heard him starting to play, I blasted some thrash metal in his direction. That soon put a stop to it. The same thing would solve your lodger problem, I reckon. After a few sessions of *The Best of Goatwhore* – highly recommended, by the way – he'll be begging to leave. And it'll drown out his coughing in the meantime.

> **Dear Dr Ozzy:**
> I work at a bank and my boss urinates with the door open. It makes me very uncomfortable. What can I do?
> Anonymous, Bakersfield, California

To be fair to your boss, when men get the call of nature, it's a very powerful urge. Our brains aren't set up to think about all of the other stuff involved, like doors, seat lids . . . or if the wall we're about to decorate is part of an important historical monument like the Alamo. Personally, I'm impressed that the guy's even making it to the bathroom. If I was stuck in a bank all day, I'd get so fucking bored that I'd be pissing out of the window, trying to hit people standing at the cash machine outside. So I really think you should give the guy a break. Better yet, next time he empties his bladder in full view of the staff, get your colleagues to give him a round of applause and a score out of ten.

> **Dear Dr Ozzy:**
> My best friend is being bullied, and he's now very depressed. He hasn't been at school for the past two

weeks. I wish I could help, but we're in different grades,
and if I don't see the bullying taking place, I can't tell a
teacher. What should I do?
David, Boston

Tell his parents. You *must* tell his parents. Bullying is a terrible thing, and it has fucked up a lot of people's lives. It's
easy to say people should just put up with it – or that it
makes you stronger – if it ain't your head being flushed
down the bog on a daily basis. My bet is that if you tell this
kid's folks, they'll be down to the school in no time to sort
it out. Do it now, before it goes too far and something
tragic happens, or you'll never forgive yourself.

Dear Dr Ozzy:
My friends tell me I'm incredibly tight-fisted.
Personally, I don't think this is fair: I just like to keep
track of my spending and try to avoid throwing away my
hard-earned cash. Should I listen to them? Are these
people even really my friends?
Jaycee, Surrey

There's a world of difference between 'careful' and 'tight as
a duck's arse'. I remember when I used to own a wine bar
and restaurant – Osbourne's, in Newport, Shropshire –
there was a bloke who was so cheap, he'd come in and
count his fucking peas. *Literally.* He'd tap me on the shoulder and say, 'How come I got seven peas and my wife got
twelve?' Then there's the kind of tightwad who claims to
be on a diet when it comes to ordering food, but then
scavenges from everyone else's plate – the 'See Food Diet',
I call it. Anyway, back to your question: if your friends are
saying they're offended by your behaviour, the chances are

you're tighter than Elvis Presley's spandex. So it can't hurt to dig deep for a while, if only to prove 'em wrong.

> **Dear Dr Ozzy:**
> Help! I just sent a long and emotional e-mail about how much I hate my job to my best friend in Sweden. But I accidentally (don't ask how) copied in my boss. What should I do?
> Margaret, New York

Start looking for a new job.

> **Dear Dr Ozzy:**
> I know you're supposed to make eye contact when talking to new people, but how far do you take it – the occasional glance (if so, how many seconds?) or a continuous full lock?
> Ken, Woking

It ain't a full lock and it ain't a glance – it's something in between. But it's very important to get it right, 'cos it's not comfortable being around people who can't look you in the eye when they're having a conversation. They always seem dodgy. Whatever you do, though, *don't* stare – if your eyes are bugging out like you're some kind of nutter, that ain't cool. It's all about giving off a warm vibe, making others feel at ease. Maybe if you stop counting how many seconds there are between every blink, it'll come naturally.

> **Dear Dr Ozzy:**
> My colleague (the next cubicle over) has terrible body odour. How can I break the news to him gently? Or is

there a way of dealing with the smell without having to
confront him?
Marie, Stoke on Trent

I take a shower ever day, so it pisses me off when other
people don't give their friends and colleagues the same
courtesy. Unfortunately, though, there's no painless answer
to your problem. You could move cubicles, I suppose. Or
put an anonymous gift of deodorant on your colleague's
desk. But the best solution is to confront him, as long as
you do it in a nice way. How about suggesting, 'Next
time you're in the bath, why don't you try turning on the
taps?'

Dear Dr Ozzy:
Excuse my French, but my boss is an arsehole. His idea
of management is to boast about every pathetic little
thing he does while belittling everyone else's
achievements. How can I get him to change his ways?
Sarah, Stoke

Why not get together with your colleagues who feel the
same way and have an intervention? Or, if it's a big company, complain to human resources (or whatever they call
it these days). Failing that, leave. That's what I used to do
when I hated a job. Or else I behaved so badly – like nick-
ing cows' eyeballs from the slaughterhouse where I worked
and putting them in girls' drinks at the pub across the
road – that they'd kick me out. Jobs are harder to find these
days, though, so that might not be the best idea.
Unfortunately, it also makes idiots like your boss think
they're God.

Dear Dr Ozzy:
A friend of mine visited my house the other day when I
was recovering from a case of winter sniffles. When he
came down with his own cold a few days after, he sent
me an angry e-mail telling me that I should have
warned him I had germs. Is this fair?
Neil, Stevenage

No. How does this guy know where he caught the cold,
anyway? Even if you *did* give it to him, what were you supposed to do, walk around in a germ-sealed plastic bag
wearing a face mask and rubber gloves? Give me a break.

Dear Dr Ozzy:
I play football after work with my colleagues, and last
week my boss broke my ankle with a dirty tackle. I'm
furious with him and want revenge – but I don't want to
get fired. Any ideas?
Guglielmo, Rome

Two words: shit happens. If you're gonna kick a ball around,
you've got to accept that some people's personalities change
beyond all recognition on the football pitch. I learned that
lesson years ago, when I played for my local pub team every
Sunday morning. Well, I say 'played' – it was really just an
excuse to air out my brain after the night before. I soon realised
that the blokes who were perfectly normal and friendly while
supping a pint at the bar turned into wild fucking animals
during a match. I mean, they forgot who they were, to the
point where they lost all self-respect. Then, five minutes later,
they would be back down the pub, as nice as you like again.
So you should forget about revenge, 'cos you can't live your
life trying to get back at people for things you should have seen

coming in the first place. Stop playing if it really bothers you. Otherwise, try to run a bit faster once your ankle's healed.

> **Dear Dr Ozzy:**
> My neighbour plays his Elton John record collection at full blast every Sunday morning – the one day of the week when I get to sleep in. No offence to Sir Elton (I know he's a friend of yours) but what can I do to banish 'Rocket Man' from my life for good?
> Adriana, Bergamo

Ask him nicely to turn it down. If that doesn't work, buy some ear-plugs – unless you want to start a feud. And let's face it, the situation could be worse. He could be playing Justin Bieber.

DR OZZY'S INCREDIBLY HELPFUL TIPS

Your Boss is an Arsehole if . . .

- He makes himself Employee of the Month ... every month.

- He docks your salary for the day you took off to go to your mum's funeral.

- He uses the stopwatch on his iPhone to time your bog breaks.

- He thinks the stopwatch on his iPhone is a 'pretty cool app'. But not as cool as the 'Pull My Finger' app – which he plays with in his office while everyone else is working their arse off.

- He gets you wasted after work, then shaves off your eyebrows when you pass out. Oh, hang on a minute . . . that was *me* . . .

- He gives you a choice between working at the weekend or giving him a blowjob.

- He promotes people based on how many times they *don't* work at the weekend.

- At a team-bonding event, he thinks it's hilarious to fire a paintball at your lovesack.

Dear Dr Ozzy:
How do you cope with people who plot against you but are as nice as pie to your face?
David, Woking

Number one: don't ever work in TV, 'cos the industry is crawling with back-stabbers. Number two: you don't have to 'cope' with them − just avoid them like the plague. Unless you're wearing handcuffs or have been slammed in a prison cell, you don't have to be in *anyone's* company (although I know it can be difficult with co-workers and bosses). I mean, if someone on the bus has BO, you don't sit next to them, do you? It's the same with people who have toxic personalities. If it's an option, get up and walk away.

Dear Dr Ozzy:
Is it just me, or is it basically impossible for men to make new friends when they're married with kids,

given that the pub is now out of bounds (at least on a regular basis)?
Chaz, Isle of Wight

That's why God invented golf and fishing. Both of these things let men get out of the house and socialise with each other without receiving a stage-five bollocking the next day. The trouble is, if you don't have the patience for any of that stuff – and I certainly don't – there ain't many other options. And it's not as if someone like me can go out for the occasional quiet pint, either. One whiff of the old devil's brew, and the next thing I know it's 4 a.m., I'm blasted to kingdom come, and I'm trying to drive my car through the front door. So, for me, the last refuge has always been the toilet. You might not make many new friends in there, but when the kids are rioting and the wife's on your case, I highly recommend it as a way of taking a quick break.

Dear Dr Ozzy:
Is it worth staying in touch with old friends – from high school, etc. – when you no longer have anything in common? Or is it better and more honest just to make a clean break?
Julian, Newport

Move on. You're a different person now from when you were a kid, so unless your old classmates have gone into the same kind of job or whatever, it's pointless going through the awkwardness of meeting up for a beer once every ten years. Having said that, it's sometimes interesting to see what became of the dickheads at school. I remember one guy who always wore the uniform (even when you didn't have to), always did his homework on time, always came top of everything. Meanwhile, I was the prankster, thief and school goldfish murderer. He ended up being a bus inspector. I became a rock star. Sometimes I have a good old chuckle about that.

> **Dear Dr Ozzy:**
> As a boss, I'm struggling to deal with a worker who's not a 'team player'. Short of firing him, which seems a bit excessive, what's the best way to manage such a difficult personality? I'm sure you have plenty of experience as the leader of a rock band.
> **David, Surrey**

I have a rule in my band: if there's something you don't like about your job, or if you've been offered a better gig somewhere else, all I ask is for a bit of notice before you leave. And it's the same in reverse. So, if I were you, I'd have a chat with this guy, tell him it ain't working out, and suggest he finds a new job by the end of the year. On the other hand, if he's doing excellent work and the only problem is that you don't like him, I'd suggest you just deal with it, 'cos talented people are hard to find, and your employees don't have to be your friends. If no one else at your company likes him either, though, that's a different matter, 'cos he'll be affecting morale. In that case, he has to go.

Dr Ozzy's Trivia Quiz:
Personal Skills

*Find the answers – and add up
your score – on page 00*

1. **How do you say hello to a close friend in northern Mozambique?**
a) Kiss them on the nose
b) Shake your fist at head level and shout, *'Wooshay! Wooshay!'*
c) Clap three times

2. **According to the etiquette people at Debrett's, during dinner you shouldn't 'glance longingly' at ...**
a) The best-looking person at the table
b) Your wife's tits
c) Your iPhone

3. **How many 'friends' does the average Facebook user have?**
a) 130
b) 95
c) 260

4. **What did a New Zealand bank manager do in 2006 that made him Worst Boss of the Year?**

a) Ordered female tellers to show at least three inches of cleavage

b) Had his staff tied up and robbed

c) Banned toilet breaks during office hours

5. **When the workers at a Lithuanian-owned car dealership in Atlanta, Georgia, asked for a pay rise, what did their boss do?**

a) Shoot them

b) Kill himself

c) Sue them for emotional distress

9

The Jelly Between Your Ears

It Ain't Easy, Being Mental

Most of us spend more time washing the dishes than we do taking care of our mental health. It's unbelievable, when you think about it, 'cos of all the things that can go wrong with us, 'not feeling yourself' is right up there with the worst. It ain't exactly rare, either. According to the World Health Organisation, one in four people come down with some kind of major freak-out at some point in their life. The trouble is, even today, people don't like to talk about it. I mean, when you go to work in the morning and the boss asks, 'How are you?' no one wants to say, 'Oh, I'm feeling a bit mentally ill today, actually.' You'd be scared of ending up in a padded room, wearing pyjamas with no fucking sleeves.

Luckily, you can always come to Dr Ozzy for advice. I've been through just about everything you can imagine:

depression, panic attacks, drug abuse, cries for help, alcohol abuse, obsessive compulsive disorder . . . you name it, man. And the one thing I've learned is that no matter how much you don't want to, you've *gotta* talk about it. Go to your GP. See a therapist. Confide in friends (although it's usually better to find someone who ain't gonna be biased). If you keep your problems bottled up, they'll only get worse over time.

Having said all that, if you grew up in England when I did, the whole idea of talking about anything was a fucking joke. If someone had any kind of anxiety or depression when I was a kid, it was called a 'nervous breakdown' – and people only ever mentioned it in hushed voices, behind closed doors. But times have changed. Treatment has improved. And people are beginning to realise that *everyone* has issues, and everyone needs to get them out in the open if they want to move on. So that's what this chapter is all about: coming clean, clearing the air, and hopefully taking the first step towards getting *real* help from someone who ain't me.

> **Dear Dr Ozzy:**
> **My friends have started to tell me that I'm way too paranoid – about my boss, my girlfriend, the government . . . you name it. Isn't a bit of paranoia good for you, though?**
> **Jamie, New York**

No. Being paranoid's a terrible way to live. For example, every so often when I get on a plane, I convince myself that it's doomed, and that we're all gonna die. So I spend the whole twelve hours in the air sweating and trying to stop my heart jumping out of my ribcage . . . which is a total waste of time, 'cos my panic attack ain't exactly gonna stop

a bomb going off or the autopilot breaking down. I suppose
you could argue that being a worrier makes you more likely
to live longer, but if you're feeling paranoid 24/7, what kind
of life are you living anyway? It ain't comfortable for the
people around you, either – especially if you're giving your
girlfriend the Gestapo interrogation treatment every time
she comes home. Listen to your mates and chill out, man.

Dear Dr Ozzy:
Can you explain why it's so bloody hard for men to cry?
Abigail, Wexham

It's not that it's hard, it's just that we don't particularly enjoy
it. I mean, yeah, every now and again – like once a
decade – a good old cry clears the air. But it ain't something your average bloke wants to do on a regular basis . . .
'cos it's exhausting. Women, on the other hand, can't seem
to get enough of it. For example, my wife insists on going
to see these awful films – 'slurpies', I call 'em – where you
spend the whole time feeling like your gran's just died. The
last one she dragged me to was *The Notebook*. By the time
the credits rolled, I was just about having a nervous breakdown. Then I thought: Why am I sitting here, in a darkened
room, feeling all unnecessarily choked up? When I looked
over at Sharon, she was even more puffy-faced and snotty
than I was. Then she goes, 'Oooh, wasn't that brilliant,
Ozzy?' At moments like that, I think that men and women
might as well be from different universes.

Dear Dr Ozzy:
I suffer from a condition known as bipolar disorder,
which makes me impulsive and harm people when I
don't mean to. It started when my father began

drinking a case of beer every night. He would get rowdy
and mean and drive me to school when he was drunk.
Now he's divorcing my sweet mom. Could this be the
cause of my problems?
Christina, Texas

I strongly suggest you find a good therapist. And by that I
mean someone who has in-depth knowledge of bipolar disorder – not just your local GP, who'll probably tell you to
take an aspirin and sleep it off. I'm not bipolar myself, but
I've been to the dark side on more than a few occasions,
and therapy has helped me a great deal over the years. It
basically gives you a different view of the things you think
might have caused your problems – like your old man's
drinking – 'cos when you're in the depths of a mental
freak-out, you often don't understand why, and you end up
blaming it on the stuff and the people around you. In other
words, you end up telling yourself that the way you *see* the
world is the way it *is* ... when, in reality, your problems
could have been caused by one of many, many things. You
might also need anti-depressants, or some other kind of
drug, but I honestly believe that therapy will be the best
treatment in your case. Or at least a good first step.

DR OZZY'S INSANE-BUT-TRUE STORIES

History's Biggest Nutters

➕ **Joan of Arc:** Cross-dressing French teenager who
led men into battle and got burned at the stake – at an
age when the worst thing most chicks have to deal with

is Bieber Fever. Some think her 'visions from God' were a symptom of bovine tuberculosis, caused by drinking unpasteurized milk. Either that, or she was fucking nuts.

➕ **Pythagoras:** Brainy Greek who loved animals and triangles. Also madder than a March hare on LSD. For example, he was totally freaked out by beans. Good job he never had to sit in a confined area with me after a burrito.

➕ **Charles the Mad:** French king who thought he was made of glass and had his trousers reinforced with iron bars in case he fell over and shattered. The guy was so mental he couldn't even remember his own name. I feel sorry for the poor fucker who had to keep reminding him: 'Your Royal Highness's name is, er ... *Charles the Mad*, sir.'

➕ **Wolfgang Amadeus Mozart:** Totally mental German composer. Now reckoned to have suffered from attention deficit disorder, bipolar disorder and Tourette's syndrome. The full title of his *Piano Concerto No. 24 in C-Minor* is actually *Piano Concerto No. 24 in C-Minor, You Fucking C****.

➕ **Lord Byron:** English poet and mad as a bag of pissed-off ferrets. Had a pet bear at college – and presumably a litterbox the size of Balmoral. Later, when he got bored of writing soppy verses, he formed his own navy and declared war on the Turks. (This is true!) Then he caught a cold and died.

Dear Dr Ozzy:
I can't control my temper. I finally realised this when I recently spent the night in jail after punching someone

in the face for 'looking at me funny'. What can I do to
calm myself down?
Graham, Yorkshire

Generally speaking, people don't just wake up angry. There's
got to be an underlying cause – something in your past, or
maybe just anxiety. Anger is a *symptom*. Beer also fuels anger.
Once, a long time ago, I hit someone with a bottle in a pub
when I was blasted out of my mind, and it still haunts me
to this day. So, if you drink, you'd better think about stopping immediately. If I were you, I'd also get some anger
management therapy. If you think that sounds like a joke
from an Adam Sandler movie, see how funny it is when you
hit someone again and get twenty years for grievous bodily
harm.

Dear Dr Ozzy:
A few months ago I was laid-off from the company I'd
been with for ten years, and although I've now found
another job – with better opportunities – I can't stop
dwelling on how I was let go, and it's making me
grumpy and depressed. Should I see a shrink?
Mark, Cleethorpes

I know exactly how you feel, Mark. I was fired by my old
band, Black Sabbath, in 1979. I mean, granted, I was a
horrendous alcoholic – but it wasn't like they were all fucking choirboys, either. Just to make things worse, it was my
best friend Bill Ward who broke the news to me. I can't
remember the specifics, 'cos I was shitfaced on beer and
cognac the day it happened, but I'll never forget how bad
it felt. After ten years, you're practically to married to what
you do for a living. When you're given the boot, it's like

going through a divorce – even if you know in your heart it's the right thing. It might be that you're just angry, in which case I would definitely recommend going to see a shrink. Otherwise, getting over it will just take time. Whatever you do, don't try to vent your frustration in other ways. In my case, I set fire to my back garden, shot all my chickens and went to the pub, but it only made me feel worse. I still feel bad for the poor chickens to this day.

Dear Dr Ozzy:
I have a terrible, gnawing sense of dread about the state of the world – in particular the environment. According to the news, this has been the wettest\ driest\hottest\coldest winter on record for just about any country you care to mention. Is this anxiety normal? Is there anything any of us can really do about it?
Carel, Dubai

Number one: stop watching the TV and browsing the internet. Number two: replace the time you've been spending doing those things with something healthier and more constructive. Me, I like to draw. Just doodles, really, but it's a great release. Don't get me wrong, I ain't saying we should all just bury our heads in the sand. But the point of the news is to keep you watching the news – so they focus on only the most horrendous stuff. If you're sensitive to it, you can literally make yourself sick. I once heard about a guy who had inoperable cancer. He went to a Chinese doctor, who told him, 'Here's what I want you to do: get rid of your TV, get rid of your radio, switch off your computer. Just focus on the positive.' After three months, he was in remission. I ain't saying he was cured by giving up *News at Ten*. But I bet it made him a lot happier.

> Dear Dr Ozzy:
> My GP recently put me on anti-depressants. Are there any side-effects I should know about?
> David, Surrey

Anti-depressants are fabulous things, David, but they'll play havoc with your meat and two veg. I've been taking them for years and while I can still get a boner, there are no fireworks. I just end up pumping away on top of Sharon like a road drill all night. I tried Viagra once, but by the time it kicked in, the missus was fast asleep. So it was just me and this tent pole in front of me, with nothing to do but watch the History Channel.

DR OZZY'S AMAZING MEDICAL MISCELLANY

Crazy, Even for Mental Disorders

🞤 **Capgras syndrome:** When you're convinced that everyone around you has been replaced with an identical imposter. If you happen to be a Third World dictator who's hired a lot of body-doubles, this might be true. For everyone else, it's a sign you need to catch the next bus to the funny farm.

🞤 **Paris syndrome:** This one affects only Japanese people. It happens when they go to Paris expecting paradise, meet the French – especially rude waiters – and can't handle it, to the point where they have a total meltdown.

The Japanese Embassy now even has a twenty-four-hour helpline for tourists who come down with it. There are usually about twenty cases a year.*

+ **Walking-corpse syndrome:** Sufferers think they're dead, and that life is a dream they're having while in heaven (or hell). I thought I had this once, but luckily it turned out I wasn't delusional because I really was dead. It was only temporary, though, while I was in a coma after my quad-bike accident.

Dear Dr Ozzy:
I keep waking up in the night after hearing loud noises, but my wife (asleep beside me) hears nothing. Could this be the so-called 'exploding head syndrome' that I once heard about on television? Or do you think it's just a common-or-garden nightmare?
Ted, Bath

Unless you've got a pet hamster who's throwing bricks out of his cage in the middle of the night, it seems unlikely that there'd be enough loud noises to make you wake up on such a regular basis. On the other hand, it's plausible that your wife could be sleeping through whatever is disturbing you. My own wife sleeps like she's been dead for twenty-five years. A Boeing 747 full of atomic bombs could crash into our back garden and she'd be none the wiser the next morning. By the sound of it, though, this is probably all in your mind. As for 'exploding head syndrome' . . . I've had

* According to www.parissyndrome.info

a few hangovers that might fit that description, but in your case it's more likely to be a bad case of anxiety dreams. Try some relaxation techniques before going to bed.

Dear Dr Ozzy:
After all the tragic shootings America, I'm curious if you think it's possible to tell in advance that a mentally ill person is going to 'snap', or if it's out of anyone's control?
Jake, Los Angeles

To me, it's not a question of being able to tell when someone's gonna snap – it's the fact that it's ridiculously easy for a crazy person to get hold of a gun in America. I mean, I should know: I'm a complete nutter, and I own several guns. All I had to do was show the guy in the shop my ID and wait a few weeks. In England, on the other hand, a copper had to come over to my house and interview me before they'd let me keep a firearm. I've got nothing against guns in general, but if the government makes people take a test before they can drive a car, why not have the same kind of rule for when you buy a Glock? They say it ain't guns that kill people, it's people who kill people ... but it would be a lot fucking harder for a lunatic to become a mass-murderer if he had to use an old frying pan instead of a semi-automatic.

Dear Dr Ozzy:
My nineteen-year-old son has started to suffer from panic attacks, usually during exams, job interviews, that kind of thing. Next week he has his driving test (third attempt) and I'm wondering if there's anything (safe) I can give him to calm him down?
Janet, Surrey

If it makes you feel any better, it took me *nineteen* attempts to pass my driving test – I finally became legal in October 2009. Not that it ever stopped me driving, mind you: if anyone ever asked me if I had a licence, I'd just say, 'Oh yes.' It was *sort of* true: I had a TV licence. About the nerves, though: I know exactly how your son feels. I used to get so intimidated by the examiner, I'd have a few of pints before getting in the car. But then I'd forget basic things, like which side of the road to drive on. Eventually I went to my GP and asked for some pills to chill me out, so he wrote me a prescription for a sedative. The box said, 'WARN-ING: DO NOT MIX WITH ALCOHOL' – so, to be safe, I smoked half a brick of Afghan hash instead. The good news: when I got into the car, I didn't feel intimated at all. The bad news: when I stopped for a red light, I nodded off. So, to answer your question: yes, there are (legal) drugs your son can take – ask your GP. But a bit of nerves is better than being too relaxed for your own good.

> **Dear Dr Ozzy:**
> You often talk about 'vibes' and 'energy', so it's clear that you feel things that other people don't. Do you think people can develop intuition, or are they just born that way?
> **Sharon, Massachusetts**

Most of the time it's just common sense. I remember when Princess Diana was still alive, for example, I woke up one morning and said to Tony, my personal assistant, 'You know what, something bad's gonna happen to her.' Sure enough, a few weeks later, she was dead. It was terribly sad. Tony said to me to later, 'Whatever you do, Ozzy, don't have any premonitions about *me*.' But the fact is, if someone's living their life at 300 m.p.h., you don't have to be a clairvoyant to see what's coming. I think some people have better intuition than others, but there ain't anything magical about it.

> **Dear Dr Ozzy:**
> I recently had to speak in public, and I was so nervous my vision became blurred. Is this 'hysterical blindness'?
> **Nicola, Cheshire**

Panic attacks can do all kinds of weird things to you – I know, 'cos I've suffered from stage fright all my life. I went to see my GP about it once and he told me, 'Try getting a brown paper bag and blowing into it.' I said, 'Apart from making my chips cool down, what the fuck is that gonna do?' He didn't take too kindly to that. I see a therapist now to treat my anxiety – it's done me a lot of good – although anything to do with your sight is so important, it might also be worth seeing an eye-doctor. The problem is that your symptoms probably appear only when you're nervous. So you might have to invite an audience and recite some Shakespeare while he checks you out.

> **Dear Dr Ozzy:**
> Every time I leave the house, I have to go back two or three times to check that the door is locked, that the oven isn't on, or that the burglar alarm is set. What's wrong with me?
> **Karen, Surrey**

A lot of people would tell you that you're 'a bit OCD' – in other words, that you've got obsessive compulsive disorder. To be honest, though, I think that might be over-egging it.

Everyone seems to have OCD these days. But worrying about leaving the door open is *normal*, especially if you have bad short-term memory, like I do. I mean, no one wants to come home and find a homeless bloke with his trousers down, taking a shit on the coffee table. But the reality is, even if you did leave the door open, the chances are nothing bad would happen. You're over-thinking things, just like I did the other night. I was home alone, and I spent the entire time crapping myself over every little rustle and creak. Then, when Sharon came back early without any warning, I just about dived under the bed for my sniper rifle. It's a good job I was too groggy to move any faster – shooting the missus would have earned me a right old bollocking.

DR OZZY'S AMAZING MEDICAL MISCELLANY

Old-Fashioned Treatments . . . to Avoid

- **Insulin coma:** Back in the day, some bright spark thought that if they shot you up with enough insulin to put you into a coma, you'd wake up cured from drug addiction and/or schizophrenia. It worked brilliantly, apart from one small problem: the 'waking up' bit. A lot of people didn't.

- **Trepanation:** If you complained about 'personal demons' in the Middle Ages, they'd strap you to a table while some fat, dribbling peasant wearing a potato sack went at your skull with a hammer and chisel. The idea was to make a big enough hole to 'let the demons out'. Unfortunately, more often than not, half your brains came out with 'em.

➕ **Hydrotherapy:** It wasn't a good idea to suffer from hyper-activity disorder, or *any* other kind of disorder, in Victorian times. You'd end up locked in the loony bin, chained to a wall, and blasted in the face with a fireman's hose until you 'calmed down'. Often the inmates calmed down to such an extent that they didn't have a pulse any more.

Dear Dr Ozzy:
I've just found out that a friend of mine is undergoing a course of electro-shock treatment for depression. It sounds terrible to me, and I want her to stop. What do you think?
Mary, Dorset

When you hear the phrase 'electro-shock treatment', you immediately think of *One Flew Over the Cuckoo's Nest*. But a very close friend of mine had this done, and apparently it's nothing like it was in the 1930s, when they basically just used to plug you into the mains and see what happened. For a start, it's called 'electroconvulsive therapy' now. All I would suggest is to ask your friend if she's absolutely sure that she's tried everything else – because, from what I understand, it's still one of those if-all-else-fails things. My friend swears that it cured her, but I've gotta say, I don't think I'd ever be miserable enough to hook myself up to one of those machines.

Dear Dr Ozzy:
Having a strict routine makes me happy – I have an OCD-type personality and anxiety – but I worry that it's

**turning me into the world's most boring person. What
should I do?**
Amelia, Boston

Sometimes you've gotta make yourself unhappy to be
happy. If you think about it, there's an up and a down to
almost everything worth doing – and the down usually
comes first. For example, I'm always horrendously anxious
before gigs, but I love the adrenaline rush I get on stage.
Maybe you need to test yourself a bit: do things that make
you feel nervous, and see if you enjoy the sense of achievement you get later. If you don't, and you're happier in bed
at 9 p.m. every night with a cup of Horlicks and a crossword, then stick to your routine. Better happy and boring
than interesting and miserable.

Dear Dr Ozzy:
**A close friend of mine has become very angry with God,
blaming Him for all his recent career, health and
romantic disappointments (of which there have been
many). Now I've read on the Internet that this is a kind
of mental disorder. Should I be worried?**
Fredo, London

Most of us are taught from birth to believe in an all-pow-
erful God with a beard who lives on a fluffy white cloud or
whatever. So, if someone's having a terrible run of luck, it
ain't exactly surprising that they can end up blaming Him.
Instead of worrying about your friend going mad – and it
certainly doesn't sound like a 'mental disorder' to me – why
not talk to him, give him a shoulder to cry on. He needs
your support, not your internet research.

Dr Ozzy's Trivia Quiz:
Grey Matter

*Find the answers – and add up
your score – on page 284*

1. **Which of these is a real mental disorder?**
a) Bigorexia
b) Foreign accent syndrome
c) Jumping Frenchman disorder

2. **If you were a hybristophiliac, what might you want to do?**
a) Marry a mass murderer
b) Have two different personalities
c) Have sex with your Toyota Prius

3. **Which of these statements about the human brain is true?**
a) There aren't any 'pain receptors' in your brain, so if Hannibal Lecter started to eat it, you wouldn't feel a thing
b) While awake, your brain generates enough power to light a 100-watt bulb
c) Music is the biggest trigger of emotional memories

4. **How many thoughts does the average person have every day (roughly)?**

a) 600
b) 70,000
c) 1 million

5. **How many prescriptions for anti-depressant drugs are handed out every year in America (estimated)?**

a) 18 million
b) 81 million
c) 118 million

10

Sex, Romance & Ballcare

Dr Ozzy's Guide to the Bats & the Bees

If you've come to the Prince of Darkness for sex advice, you're already in big fucking trouble. It ain't that I don't have a lot of experience in the bedroom department – I've got my fair share of war stories, like any other rocker – it's just that I wasn't conscious for most of it. Back in the 1970s, most chicks used to light up a cigarette after a good old bonk. Not the ones I slept with: they were too busy calling for an ambulance.

Still, I've picked up a few pearls of wisdom here and there, which is a good job, 'cos at least half of the questions I get are from people with sex problems . . . or romance problems . . . or ball problems. Or, more often than you'd think, a combination of all three. To make things easy, I've rolled them all into this chapter. Just remember: there's more to life than mind-blowing sex. And if you find out what it is, let me know.

SEX

Dear Dr Ozzy:
When my girlfriend takes Ambien, she turns into an
insatiable sexual freak. In the morning, though, she has
no memory of it. Is it wrong for me to go along with
this?
Rob, California

It sounds like I need to send my missus' Ambien back to
the pharmacy and ask for a refund: when Sharon takes it,
she turns into an insatiable fucking snorer, not a sexual
freak. Having said that, if your girlfriend doesn't remember
any of these epic rogerings in the morning, it seems you're
getting dangerously close to date-rape. Aside from the fact
that it ain't right, if she ever found out about it, and you
had an argument and broke up, you could end up in leg-
irons and a jumpsuit. I think a confession is in order.

Dear Dr Ozzy:
I gave my wife a vibrator as a gift. Now, every night
when she thinks I'm asleep, I can hear her using it next
to me. We're barely having sex, and I'm worried I can't
compete with the machine. Please help.
Anonymous (no address given)

Hide the batteries.

Dear Dr Ozzy:
I've been sleeping on and off with an average-looking
girl at work for a few months – usually after a Friday-

night session in the pub. Yesterday I found out she's
updated her 'relationship status' on Facebook and is
calling me her boyfriend! I never wanted this to become
serious. How can I tell her this without causing drama?
Jeff, Preston

First of all, you've got a lot of balls calling this girl 'average-
looking'. What are *you*, Mr fucking Brad Pitt? Second, if you
go to bed with a girl more than once, you either have to be
a man and explain to her that it ain't serious – and run the
risk of her not shagging you any more – or stop doing it,
'cos she's gonna get hurt. You also need to ask yourself
the question: 'How would I feel if this were the other way
around?' I mean, men are very good at saying, 'Oh, it's
nothing, just the occasional shag,' but if another bloke
comes on the scene, they're like wild animals marking their
territory. Make up your mind about how you feel, then
stop messing this poor girl around.

Dear Dr Ozzy:
I have a policy of not advising people on their love lives.
However, I suspect my friend 'Bob' (not his real name)
might be having an extra-marital relationship with a
neighbour, largely because he likes her breasts. If this
was your mate, would you offer advice?
John, Aberdeen

No. Trust me – stay away. It's impossible to know all the
facts in these situations, and you probably wouldn't want to.
Meanwhile, if he ever asks you to start covering for him,
just say, 'What you do is none of my business, but don't ever
ask about this again, 'cos I don't want to know.' Otherwise,
you're putting your head in the lion's mouth, and sooner or

later, two slobbering jaws are gonna come chomping down on your neck – I guarantee it. The only time you'd have any reason to pipe up would be if someone was getting hurt, or if the situation became horrendous – like he started bringing his bit on the side over to your house for dinner. In that case, it would be worth having a quiet word.

> Dear Dr Ozzy:
> Why do men always want young girlfriends? Young people are boring: they don't have good stories to tell or interesting views to share. Do men think only with their trousers?
> Darla, Helsinki

The truth is that men have *two* brains: the one in their heads and the one in their Y-fronts. And the second one usually wins – that's why you see guys with bald spots and pony tails walking around Los Angeles. A sixty-three-year-old friend of mine came over to my house the other day in his sports car with some young female in the passenger seat who might as well have been his great-granddaughter. I said to him, 'Where do you find these girls? Mothercare?' He just laughed. But I guarantee it won't make him happy for long, 'cos one day they'll be lying in bed and he'll want to talk about Colonel Gaddafi, and she'll think he's talking about the guy who invented fried chicken. (In response to this question, a guy called Peter from West Sussex wrote in to say: 'Ask Darla from Helsinki why men should *not* have young girlfriends. I sail, ski, work out three days a week, and prefer slim and energetic companions to my overweight, TV-watching contemporaries. PS: I am eighty-one years old.')

Dear Dr Ozzy:
How do you make a girl reach orgasm?
Andre, St Albans

I've always been too busy giving *myself* an orgasm to pay much attention. But if you find out, let me know.

Dear Dr Ozzy:
I'm a twenty-eight-year-old woman who has never – not once! – reached orgasm. I enjoy sex, but it's more like a good aerobic workout than something mind-blowing. Am I choosing the wrong guys or do I have some kind of deep psychological handicap? Please help.
Sanna, Helsinki

Dr Ozzy is a bit out of his depth on this one (see above), but the first thing to do is look at the side-effects of any pills you're taking. For example, anti-depressants wreak havoc in my own screaming ecstasy department – but I don't know what the deal is for women. Maybe also buy one of those electronic 'back massagers', then try to get yourself over-the-top on your own. The better you know your own body, the better chance you have of learning what sets you off. Failing that . . . give me a call.

Dear Dr Ozzy:
After I have sex, my feet tingle. What's happening? Bad circulation? Return of blood to my feet?
Daniel, New Hampshire

Let me ask you something: are you one of those blokes who likes to wear ladies' underwear? Because I once knew a girl who wore tights during a game of hide-the-sausage, and her feet fell asleep halfway through. Maybe that's your problem. Either that or get rid of the ropes and the ball gag, and don't do it hanging upside down next time.

> Dear Dr Ozzy:
> My boyfriend and I have been together for a long time.
> To spice up our sex life, he's suggested a threesome
> with one of his college mates. Does this make him gay?
> Anonymous (no address given)

Call me a boring old turd, but I've always preferred sex when it's done on a one-at-a-time basis. With more than one dick swinging around the place, you might end up with a black eye or – God forbid – getting one of 'em stuck in the wrong place. To answer your question, though: to me, it sounds more like your boyfriend's bi, not gay. Then again, his buddy might be gay. You could spend the evening with nothing to do but watch two hairy blokes going at it hammer and tongs, which wouldn't be much fun for you. Alternatively, what if you end up liking the other guy more than your boyfriend? Trust me, threesomes might look good on telly, but they're usually more trouble than they're worth.

> Dear Dr Ozzy:
> My friend and I – both married men – have been
> reliving old times by going out drinking and chatting up
> women, but stopping before any actual infidelity takes
> place. We call them 'dry runs', because they give us the
> thrill of the chase without breaking any rules. Is this
> wrong?
> Michael, London

Playing with matches is a lot of fun, Michael, but at some point your wig's gonna catch fire. There's just no way this can end well for you. One night you'll have too many drinks, you'll do a 'dry run' on a beautiful, single woman, she'll make the first move, and before you know it, you'll be signing your divorce papers. You're creating temptation for yourself, which means trouble is only two steps ahead. Get a lapdance if you're desperate for a quick thrill – or, better yet, take the missus away for a dirty weekend.

DR OZZY'S INSANE-BUT-TRUE STORIES

If You Think *Human* Sex is Weird ...

- When a male bee, or drone, gets lucky, his balls literally *fall off* inside the virgin queen. This stops her getting knocked up by any other drones. It also hurts.

- If you think human blokes have it bad, spare a thought for male giraffes. For starters, sex is limited to a two-week period each year (the only time females are up for it). And it ain't exactly much to look forward to anyway: before any action takes place, the female has to make absolutely sure that her mate is 'Mr Right', which she does by pissing on his face.

- Female hyenas don't just wear the trousers in their relationships – they even get boners. That's 'cos they have a 'pseudopenis', which is basically a massive clitoris. I bet they have hairy armpits, too.

- Male bedbugs have gotta be the biggest bastards in the sex department. Instead of courting the female, or even bothering to come up with a decent chat-up line, he just stabs her in the chest with his spiky dick. Biologists call it 'traumatic insemination'. It's just fucking lazy, if you ask me.

Dear Dr Ozzy:
I have an annoying habit of popping the champagne cork before the party gets under way. I've tried slowing down and/or mentally re-tiling the kitchen to take my mind off things during the process, but no luck, alas. Any advice would be gratefully received.
Jezz, Hertfordshire

Is this code for something? This is Dr Ozzy you're writing to, not the fucking Archbishop of Canterbury, so you don't need to get all Bletchley Park on me. If you mean what I *think* you mean, why not just get on with it quicker? It'll give you and the missus more time to do the garden.

Dear Dr Ozzy:
I have just turned sixty-eight and have the opposite problem to your premature 'cork popper'. It doesn't matter how racy my thoughts are – say, Jennifer Aniston in a maid's outfit – I still end up pumping away when the missus is ready for a cigarette. What can I do?
Dave, Wales

They have a word for this: 'anorgasmia'. There's another term for it, too: 'being sixty-eight years old'. Unfortunately, as blokes get on a bit, *everything* to do with sex becomes difficult. If it's any consolation, the most exciting thing that happens in my bedroom most nights is an episode of *Law & Order*. Having said that, you should get your prostate checked out, and ask your doctor about the side-effects of any drugs you're taking. Of course, you could also just be bored. Try thinking about Courtney Cox in a nurse's uniform instead.

> Dear Dr Ozzy:
> I have an embarrassing fetish (although I hear it's surprisingly common). I want my girlfriend to put me in a diaper and treat me like a big baby. My girlfriend and I are compatible in every way, but I'm terrified to ask her about this. What would you do?
> Anonymous (no address given)

This one's a bit far out, even for Dr Ozzy. I mean, there'll be plenty of opportunities later in life to wear nappies, so why speed up the process? Having said that, I had the opposite problem from yours during my drinking days: Sharon was always *telling* me to wear nappies, 'cos I used to piss in the bed so often. I also used to shit my pants on a fairly regular basis, which ain't very fucking nice. I suppose if you start doing the same thing, your girlfriend might make the same suggestion, saving you a tricky conversation.

> Dear Dr Ozzy:
> I'm twenty-nine years old and have become increasingly dependent on seriously hardcore porn to get turned on. Is this going to ruin my performance with real women?
> Anonymous (no address given)

No. Women didn't stop getting knocked up when the internet was invented – although maybe their husbands don't
pester them for sex as much now that they've got access to
online filth twenty-four hours a day. The trouble is, even
the XXX stuff gets boring very quickly: it's not like there's
ever a surprise fucking ending. The trick is to ration your
exposure, not try to find stronger and stronger stuff. If it
ever gets to the point where there's crapping or donkeys
involved, I think we can safely say you've gone too far.
Otherwise, stop worrying.

> **Dear Dr Ozzy:**
> I've just returned from a brilliant stag weekend in Las
> Vegas. Being married with kids, however, I'm
> concerned that the stripper with whom I, er, 'relaxed' in
> a private booth might have given me oral herpes. We
> didn't do anything improper, but she did feed me
> strawberries and cream, mouth to mouth. Any words of
> wisdom?
> **Brian, Warrington**

Forget oral herpes, Brian. It sounds to me like you've come
down with a classic case of married man's guilt. That's the
problem with strippers: they don't just take your dough,
they also make you feel like the worst husband in the world
the next morning. And if you think strippers are bad, try
groupies: I used to get so out of my mind with guilt, I'd be
down to the doctor's office every day of the week, thinking I had some new disease. Then I'd finally break down,
tell Sharon everything, and get a house plant over the back
of my head – which meant another visit to the doctor. As
for the good old herpes: your GP will give you a test to see
if you've got it, but the virus can lie dormant for years, so

there'd be no telling if you caught it from the stripper or, say, from an unwashed glass you picked up in a pub. I used to get outbreaks myself when I was stressed out or tied, but I haven't had one for years. One thing I wouldn't recommend is confessing all to your missus. Believe me, it'll only make your life worse.

> **Dear Dr Ozzy:**
> Out of the blue, my husband has suggested bringing
> another woman into our bedroom – to liven things up a
> bit after twenty years of marriage. I'm not keen. What
> do you think?
> Susan, Dundee

Sounds fair enough to me – as long as what's good for the goose is good for the gander. If your husband gets to bring Debbie from Accounts to bed, then you should be able to bring along Dave from Marketing. But that raises the obvious fucking question: if you both want to sleep with other people in your own home, what are you still doing together?

> **Dear Dr Ozzy:**
> I've noticed that I can't last as long in bed with my
> girlfriend as I could when we first started going out
> with each other three months ago. Now I'm worried
> that if I don't fix this, she might leave me for someone
> who can fully please her. Any advice?
> Ethan (no address given)

Send her to me! Seriously though, Ethan, this kind of thing is a big problem when you're a rock star. I remember one time when me and the guys from Black Sabbath were staying at a Holiday Inn in America, *three* groupies came to my room – one after the other. You'd have to be superhuman not to run out of steam during a session like that, especially after number two (and it's not like there was any Viagra around in those days). Fortunately, I was a young man, so I activated the Special Reserve Tank and finished the job. But you've gotta bear in mind that was just *one* wild night, which ain't exactly the same as a long-term relationship. When a woman becomes your steady girlfriend, it's natural that things simmer down a bit over time. Wait until you're married: you'll be in and out within five minutes while your missus is still doing the crossword.

> Dear Dr Ozzy:
> A friend recently showed me some photos on his mobile of him boning a very hot girl. The problem is that the girl is also a good friend of mine. Should I tell her what he's doing or keep my mouth shut? I guess what I'm asking is: are you a 'bros before hos' kinda guy?
> Sean, New York

Send me the pictures and I'll decide. Seriously, though, this ain't a question of some bullshit code of male honour. If she's a friend, and you want her to stay your friend, tell her. Simple as that.

> Dear Dr Ozzy:
> I'm fifty-four years old and sex mad. Does the lust ever fade?
> Pete, Fife

If you're a red-blooded man, I firmly believe that the only time you'll ever get any peace from down below is when you're in the ground. Until then, the second brain below your waist is gonna be making its own decisions, whether you like it or not. I mean, I'm sixty-two, and I still love a good old game of 'Where's the salami?' Getting anyone to play it with me is another matter entirely, though. Luckily, as you get older, your memory goes, so even if you see a sexy woman and start to feel randy, you can't remember what it was you were excited about five minutes later. That makes things a lot easier.

Dear Dr Ozzy:
What's the nicest way to let a girl know she smells bad,
especially, uh, y'know ... 'down there'?
Ron, Indiana

Try throwing up. As they say, actions speak louder than words.

Dear Dr Ozzy:
Is it ever acceptable for a married man to get a lap
dance at a strip club?
Louise, Morecambe

If you're gonna tell your wife about it — *no*. If you're not gonna tell your wife about it — *yes*. But they're stupid places, strip clubs. I know people who spend most of their lives in them, like kids in a toy shop. I've never seen the attraction, personally. I mean, every female performer in a titty joint has been up close and personal with about ten other guys that night. How is that a turn on? If someone's so desperate to see a pair of naked breasts, I suggest they buy a copy of the *Sun* and save five hundred quid.

Dear Dr Ozzy:
I'm a twenty-eight-year-old virgin (ouch). I recently met
a girl and we tried to make love – but I couldn't finish.

She accused me of indulging in solitary pleasures and wearing out 'the big chap'. Is this possible? We tried again in the morning but my problems just got worse, and I couldn't even achieve match fitness. What's wrong with me?
Chris, Reading

This could just be nerves, Chris. Also, if you were drinking before your first attempt, that might have stopped you from reaching the fireworks ceremony. Then again, maybe you *are* 'wearing out the big chap' − it's not like you're denying it, are you? So, my advice is calm down, don't drink beforehand . . . and cut out the five-knuckle shuffles.

Dear Dr Ozzy:
My husband − a builder − has always enjoyed it when I'm dominant in the bedroom, but the other day he asked me to call him a 'good little girl' while we were making love. Should I be worried or do all men have weird fantasies?
Jill, Huddersfield

Look, a lot of blokes have strange things that get them going, but this one's a bit of a cause for alarm, don't you think? I mean, if Sharon asked me to start calling her a 'big bad boy' in the bedroom, I'd probably jump out of the fucking window, screaming. Having said that, if you don't mind saying it, and he enjoys hearing it, then good luck to you both. Just make sure you keep a close eye on your underwear drawer, 'cos my guess is that when you leave the house in the morning, your mister probably becomes a missus . . .

Dear Dr Ozzy:
I'm in a serious relationship, but I've been thinking
about going to one of those 'rub'n'tug' massage
parlours. Given that a) my girlfriend will never know, b)
there's no chance of picking up an STD, and c) it doesn't
seem wrong, is there any reason I shouldn't?
Jacob, Riverside, California

A handjob is a very personal thing, and after a lifetime of
practice, most blokes get a pretty fucking specific prefer-
ence for the kind of technique they like. So, unless you're
acting as a co-pilot and barking out instructions to your
dodgy masseuse every two seconds, it might end up feeling more like she's skinning a dead rabbit than driving you
wild with forbidden pleasure. In fact, it sounds to me like
you've already built this up in your head to the point where
it's bound to be an expensive disappointment. You also ain't
factored in guilt. It's all very well telling Dr Ozzy that 'it
doesn't seem wrong' to hire an extra pair of hands to help
out in the monkey-spanking department, but if you're anything like me, your conscience won't agree.

ROMANCE

Dear Dr Ozzy:
My girlfriend bites my lip when we kiss. She thinks this
is sexy, but it really hurts. It's so bad now, I try to avoid
snogging her. How can I tell her this without hurting
her feelings and/or looking like a wimp who can't take
a bit of rough foreplay?
Giles, Fulham

Say to her: 'If you're hungry, I'll get you a sandwich.'
Seriously, though, you ain't a wimp for not wanting to go
to bed with Jaws every night. I've never understood people
who get off on being in pain. I mean, life's hard enough
as it is, so why turn the simple pleasure of getting your
end away into something that involves ball gags and
piano wire? Try biting her back, and see how *she* likes it.
(Although, if it turns her on, you might have an even bigger
problem.)

> **Dear Dr Ozzy:**
> My boyfriend hates all the television shows I watch, and
> when he criticises them (loudly and every night), it
> makes me feel like an idiot for wanting a bit of
> mindless distraction after a hard day at work. Does this
> mean I should break up with him?
> Katy, Somerset

If couples broke up 'cos they didn't like the same kind of
telly, the divorce rate would quadruple overnight. Men's
and women's brains are wired differently, so the chances are
you ain't gonna want to watch a documentary on Gulf War
tanks, and he ain't gonna want to watch some slurpy tear-
jerker or a makeover show. You could take it in turns to
watch your favourite shows; buy a second telly; or sit
down, make a list of the stuff you both enjoy, and program
the DVR accordingly. As for your boyfriend making you
feel like an idiot – he probably just thinks he's as entitled as
you are to relax with something he enjoys after a hard day
at work. And I've gotta admit, I'm guilty of the same thing.
I'm always saying to Sharon, 'You ain't watching *that* fucking crap again, are you?'

Dear Dr Ozzy:
As a thirty-year-old devoutly religious Roman Catholic
virgin, I am finally considering playing the field until I
find that special someone in my life. Is this morally and
socially acceptable in the modern world?
Ryan, County Armagh

I think it's very admirable to hold out that long, 'cos it's so
rare these days. At the same time, I have to say if hadn't
been laid by the time I was your age, I'd be asking myself,
'What's wrong?' I was just fifteen when I lost my virginity,
and I was so randy it felt like my Y-fronts were about to
explode. Another problem with holding out is that if you
do finally marry someone, what happens if you discover
that you don't like making love to them? You don't want to
marry for lust, either, 'cos you'll spend more time washing
the dishes with your other half than you will between the
sheets. So, my prescription for you is to have one bonk,
three times a day, for two weeks. Doctor's orders.

Dear Dr Ozzy:
My girlfriend and I are talking about marriage. She's
awesome, except for one thing: she gives the world's
worst head. I mean, really bad. Is this a good enough
reason to move on and find another wife? A life of sub-
par BJs seems like a life not worth living.
Guy, Colorado

Look, I know blowjobs are quite nice, but there *is* more to
life. And there's always a trade-off – for men *and* women.
You could dump this girl and end up with a fiancée who's
amazing at blowjobs but smells like a three-day-old fucking haddock. More importantly, Miss Fellatio USA might

be a royal pain in the arse, may well never help around the house, and could end up going down on your best mate while you're away on a business trip. Why not think of something you're girlfriend's *good at*, and concentrate on that?

> **Dear Dr Ozzy:**
> I have a rather pushy, much older, single (unattractive) neighbour who has strongly hinted at us having a romantic relationship. I'm not interested in the slightest, but he's not getting the message, and every time I pass him in the street he races up to me. He's also started to become (inappropriately) touchy-feely. I don't want to fall out with him – he's my neighbour – but short of sprinting away when I see him, do I have any other option?
> Katie (no address given)

It sounds to me like he's the kind of bloke who won't give up, no matter what you say, so if you've already tried the nice way, now's the time to tell him, 'Look, what part of "fuck off" don't you understand?' I mean, no one wants to fall out with their neighbours, but at the same time, you don't want to be creeping out of your own front door and diving into the hedge if you see him coming. Why should you have to live like that, when you're not the one with the problem? Make it clear: 'There's no chance, there never will be a chance, and if you touch me again, I'll take out a restraining order!'

> **Dear Dr Ozzy:**
> I've just finished college and moved back in with my mom . . . but now I've developed feelings for her

(younger) boyfriend, to the point where we flirt and hang out all the time. Should I come clean with my mom or leave it alone? I didn't mean for this to happen!
Katy, Oklahoma

You do realise that it's every bloke's fantasy to get a mother *and* her daughter into the sack, don't you? Check out the internet if you don't believe me. I mean, if this bloke gets into your pants after humping your mum, he's gonna be bragging about it for the rest of his life. If you're okay with that, sleep with him. If you'd rather have true love, then you should come clean about what's going on to your mum – and kick this creep out of the house.

DR OZZY'S INCREDIBLY HELPFUL TIPS

Rules of Romance

➕ **Guys:** When trying to get your partner into the sack, avoid phrases like 'meat thermometer', 'one-eyed yogurt slinger' and 'cheesy bratwurst'. At least until you're married.

➕ **Girls:** They say a home-cooked meal is the way to a man's heart. So are blowjobs, and they take a lot less time. You won't need a Jamie Oliver cookbook, either.

➕ **Guys:** *Always* pay. Or steal, and pretend you paid.★

➕ **Girls:** Always *offer* to pay, even if you'd dump the guy in a heartbeat if he accepted.

★ Might not be legal where you live.

> ✚ **Both sexes:** Make sure you buy little gifts for your part-
> ner at unexpected moments. That way, when you forget
> their birthday, you'll get less of a bollocking.

Dear Dr Ozzy:
I finally married my girlfriend last year after a decade
together. Now she wants kids (her clock is ticking!), but
I'm terrified by the thought. What should I do?
Anonymous (no address given)

Get a dog. That should buy you a year or so. To be brutally
honest, though, you should have thought about what she
wanted before putting a ring on her finger. Now you've
gotta be a man and live with the consequences. And who
knows? Maybe you'll enjoy being a dad.

Dear Dr Ozzy:
My girlfriend hasn't had sex with me for months – she's
always too tired after work. Is our relationship dead?
What can I do to make her interested in a game of hide
the sausage?
Adam, Brooklyn

Romance, Adam. You need a bit of romance. That includes
not using phrases like 'hide the sausage'. As I've always
said to Sharon, there are twenty-four hours in a day, so it
shouldn't be so hard to make sure you spend at least one of
them with each other. Go on a date. Have dinner together.
Or put on a wig and a false beard, check into a B&B, and
shag the shit out of each other, like you're having an affair.

Maybe the fact that she isn't going to bed with you is a form of protest. Maybe she just wants more excitement in her life.

> **Dear Dr Ozzy:**
> My boyfriend and I have split up a few times but keep getting back together – we can't live apart! Recently, though, the excitement we had six months ago has vanished (especially for him). If ending it all isn't an option, how can we get the spark back?
> Mary (seventeen years old), Kent

Listen: at the age of seventeen, your excitement level is gonna be going up and down like a fiddler's elbow. Just give it some time. Most teenage relationships don't last. Then again, I've known people who met each other at your age and lived happily ever after for the rest of their lives. (I've also known people who lived together for ten years, got married, then immediately got divorced.) The important thing is always to be yourself. If your boyfriend doesn't find that exciting enough, then, believe me, he ain't worth the effort.

> **Dear Dr Ozzy:**
> After about a year of dating my girlfriend, I've finally realised that I enjoy jerking off more than sleeping with her. Is this fucked up? Should I break the news to her?
> Scott, Connecticut

Let's face it, it's hard to beat a good old five-knuckle shuffle. For a start, you don't have to take your right hand out for dinner before it'll get down to business. It also doesn't care if you last five minutes or five seconds. And it ain't gonna demand an earth-shaking climax of its own. Admitting this to your girlfriend is a whole different thing, though. If she's anything like my own wife, I would advise against it — unless you want to be kicked so hard in the balls that you won't be able to knock one out again for the next ten years.

> **Dear Dr Ozzy:**
> I have been with my beautiful wife for twenty years, and our sex life has always been wonderful. But instead of making love every day, like we used to, it's now just two or three times a week. I'm starting to worry if it's me or her – and if, as I'm getting older, my desire is fading (I'm sixty-five). Please help, this is such a huge part of my life.
> **Howard, London**

Three times a week — at the age of *sixty-five*?! Come back to me when it's three times a *year*. Seriously, man . . . you ain't in a bad place. You need to enjoy yourself while you still can and stop moaning.

> **Dear Dr Ozzy:**
> I'm a forty-two-year-old single man who lives with his mother. Worse than that, I'm a bedwetter. I'm convinced it's the reason why I've never had the confidence to ask a girl out on a date. Please help.
> **Terry, Lancaster**

As I've said before, I used to be a bedwetter when I was still drinking. Sharon would have to put on a life-jacket when she went to sleep at night. It wasn't just the bed, either: I'd take a leak in the wardrobe, over the edge of the balcony, in the fridge-freezer, you name it. Eventually, I went to my doctor and said, 'Look, I don't want to piss the bed, but I don't want to stop drinking, either.' He told me, 'You can have one or the other, not both.' So, if you're a drinker: stop. In the meantime, go and see your GP. You ain't gonna tell him anything he ain't heard before, and this is worth checking out.

> Dear Dr Ozzy:
> One of my old boyfriends (he dumped me) has just become engaged to a very wealthy, very good-looking and very well-known French woman. I know it's not healthy, but I'm obsessing over it. In your experience, what's the best cure for a jealous heart?
> Katherine, Rugby

You could always do what I did when I was dumped by a girl at Silver Blades ice rink in Birmingham: I got the word out to her friends that I was so upset, I was gonna emigrate to Australia (it was a ten-quid offer they were promoting in the travel agent's at the time). It was all bullshit: I didn't even have ten pence in those days, never mind ten quid. But she had me back anyway. Then I realised I'd never liked her that much to begin with. That's the funny thing with jealousy: it's not about wanting something 'cos it'll make you happy. It's about wanting something 'cos you've been told you can't have it.

> Dear Dr Ozzy:
> My ex-boyfriend left me for my best friend last summer. Just to rub salt in the wound, I recently found out that he proposed a year to the day after breaking up with me. I'm now considering sending them a steaming

bag of shit as a wedding gift. Should I do this, or let
karma run its course?
Ashley, New Jersey

Think of it this way, Ashley: your steaming bag of shit *is* his
karma. Having said that, if you're gonna send crap in the
mail, take a leaf out of my wife's book, and do it right:
put it in a ziplock bag inside of a Tiffany's box. Everyone
loves to get a Tiffany's box – which makes the thought of
them untying the ribbon and bow to find a fresh dump
inside even more satisfying.

Dear Dr Ozzy:
A really good friend of mine went on a couple of dates
with a very minor celebrity. Each time it felt like a
Bachelor episode, because he never made a move. Now,
a month later – under a lot of pressure – he's confessed
he has herpes. She still wants to date him, but in my
opinion he can't be trusted. Who's right here?
Diana, California

Are you absolutely *sure* he has herpes? I might be wrong,
but I don't think most guys would mention the H-word at
all – especially not after two dates – unless they had a raging
attack of it that was making their balls glow fluorescent
green. To me, it seems like he might be using it as an
excuse to cover up an even deeper secret. You never know:
maybe he has a boyfriend on the side and doesn't want to
sleep with your friend at all.

Dear Dr Ozzy:
I'm a heterosexual man – honestly – but I've found myself
becoming stimulated in the most embarrassing way

while getting a Swedish rub-down from a male masseur.
Even worse: it was a couples massage, and my wife was
lying next to me. She noticed ... and hasn't talked to me
since. What can I say to her to make this better?
Eric, Melrose

Oh, Eric. You could always say, 'I've never kissed a man –
but I might have kissed a man who has.' Seriously, though,
I suppose the question is: would your wife have been more
or less pissed off if you'd reacted in the same way to a female
masseuse? If you think she might have been cooler with it,
you could always tell her it was the thought of a *ménage à
trois* that set you off, not the big glistening hunk of love
muscle who was stimulating your deep tissue. Actually, no,
don't do that. All I can say is that, in future, you might want
to try avoiding other blokes when you're down the parlour.
Personally, I couldn't think of anything more uncomfortable
than being oiled down by some ex-Chippendale while
Kenny G plays in the background. Don't get me wrong:
I ain't got anything against the gay community. But when
someone says the word 'Swedish' to me, I think Ulrika
Jonsson ... not Björn Borg.

Dear Dr Ozzy:
I'm still 'friends with benefits' with my ex-boyfriend,
even though he now has a new girlfriend – the same
girl he cheated on me with for almost a year and a half.
Should I tell her what the hell has been going on, since
he hasn't had the balls to be honest?
Rudy, South Carolina

If you're looking for revenge, go ahead. But don't kid
yourself – it sounds like this is a play to get him back. You

might also want to consider that if he's cheated on you, and is now cheating on her, he's probably screwing a few other people, too. I mean, the bloke doesn't exactly sound like the faithful type. My advice would be to find a new guy and move on.

> Dear Dr Ozzy:
> My girlfriend's father – Russian, ex-military – likes to get me drunk on vodka then take me to his *banya* (sauna), where we strip naked and he whips me with birch leaves. Is this weird?
> Adam, New York

If some bird's dad ever tried to get me naked so he could whip me with something – birch twigs or otherwise – he'd get a punch in the fucking conk. Getting boozed up in a sauna ain't a very clever idea, either . . . although I used to do it all the time at my old house in Staffordshire. I took precautions, mind you: before putting any water on the coals, I'd always top up my lager with a splash of lemonade. One other thing, Adam: generally speaking, any kind of physical activity in hot, steamy conditions is best avoided, unless you're using the sauna to have a quickie with the nanny (another thing I once did, long ago). In that case, an exception can be made.

> Dear Dr Ozzy:
> I wish my girlfriend were better endowed. Would it be rude to suggest a boob job? (I'd pay for it.)
> Stan, Cheshire

The good thing about being Dr Ozzy is that I sometimes get the opportunity to save lives. Stan, count yourself lucky, 'cos that's what I'm about to do: under *no* circumstances *ever* bring this up with your girlfriend. If I made this suggestion to Sharon, believe me, the Osbourne crown jewels would soon be halfway up my oesophagus. And, to be honest, I wouldn't blame her. I mean, imagine if the situation were reversed, and your girlfriend asked you to get an enlargement of your own? How would *you* feel? If it's really that important to you, dump the girl and find yourself a Page 3 model.

> **Dear Dr Ozzy:**
> **What's the best way to make a woman sleep with you?**
> **Jake, New York**

I always had a great chat-up line for women. After a night out, I'd say, 'Can I come back to your house and watch your telly?' I thought it was brilliant, 'cos it made it sound like all I wanted to do was catch *News at Ten*, when in fact I was planning to get them into the sack. No one ever fell for it, though. Most of the time, they just said, 'I ain't got a telly.'

BALLCARE

> **Dear Dr Ozzy:**
> **This might sound strange, but I've noticed that when I stare at my testicles for a long time, they seem to move all by themselves. Is this normal? It's freaking me out!**
> **Jason (thirteen years old), Kent**

It's normal. If they start moonwalking, you might have a problem, but they definitely move on their own, 'cos they're surrounded by a layer of jelly and, as everyone who's ever looked at a bowl of jelly knows, it tends to wobble around for no good reason. On a separate note, though: you might want to spend less time staring at your testicles.

Dear Dr Ozzy:
The skin on my penis has cracked due to (solo) over-use. Is this normal? If so, how can I make it heal?
Anonymous, New York

It's called friction. Rub the skin on your elbow ten times a day and you'll have exactly the same problem. Give your upstanding citizen a break for a while, then invest in some 'personal lubrication'.

Dear Dr Ozzy:
I've been contacted by a very friendly woman on the internet who tells me that 'male enhancement' surgery – i.e., phalloplasty – is risk-free and guaranteed to make me a hero in bed. Should I proceed?
Larry, California

No. Next question . . .

Dear Dr Ozzy:
I'm an uncircumcised sixteen-year-old and can't retract my foreskin. I'm stressing out about it, but can't face going to a doctor (which would mean telling my parents). What can I do?
Mark, Birmingham

First of all, under no circumstances start messing around with it yourself. Second, I appreciate that it's embarrassing, but the best thing to do is have a quiet word with your dad, or an older brother, if you've got one. Bear in mind that your old man probably changed a few of your nappies when you were little, so you ain't showing him anything he hasn't seen plenty of times already. The same goes for your doctor: believe me, people have far worse problems than a sticky foreskin (which I reckon has gotta be pretty common). Just pluck up the courage and get it over with, 'cos it'll seem like nothing as soon as it's done.

DR OZZY'S AMAZING MEDICAL MISCELLANY

What Every Man Should Know ...

- 'Blue balls' is a *real* condition. It's a kind of cramp that happens when you have a woody for a long time but never get to the fireworks display. Interestingly, no female in medical history has *ever* accepted 'blue balls' as a good reason for a bonk.

- The average guy gets an average of five boners every night. If the average guy is anything like me, he also gets an average of zero shags.

- One ejaculation contains up to 400 million sperm. I'm guessing it was a woman who counted 'em afterwards, 'cos the bloke would have been fast asleep.

- With quick treatment, the survival rate for testicular cancer is about 95 per cent. The trick is to check your balls regularly for lumps. Don't do it during business meetings or when you're in a posh restaurant, though.

Dear Dr Ozzy:
I've heard that regular ejaculations are important to keep the prostate healthy as one gets older. As there is a history of prostate cancer in my family, would a regular 'cleaning out of the system' be a good idea, purely from a health point of view? If so, how often?
Andy, Beaconsfield

You're absolutely right, Andy. I recommend a vigorous spring cleaning once a day. It's best done in private, but if you're caught, just mention the words 'preventative medicine' and you'll be fine.

Dear Dr Ozzy:
I saw a yellow spongy froth come out of my fifty-four-year-old boyfriend's penis during ejaculation. He says it's been three years since he had sex. Could it be 'rusty pipes'? I'm a thirty-eight-year-old woman, and I've seen a lot – but I've never seen *that* before!
Haydee, New York

Listen, Haydee: if I had yellow spongy frothy shit coming out of my dick, I wouldn't be writing to Dr Ozzy – I'd be running to the fucking hospital! It's a cause for alarm, don't you think? It reminds me of when I was younger, and this school friend of mine started to piss sperm. You ain't never seen anything like it. We were all looking at him, our jaws on the floor, going, 'Is this what happens when you reach thirteen? Is that his life supply – *gone*?' I've no idea what happened to that kid, but I hope he got it checked out. Back to your question: you could always get your boyfriend to knock a few out by himself, to see if the problem really is 'rusty pipes'. Personally, though, I'd be making a date with my local dick doctor – and not wasting any time about it, either.

> **Dear Dr Ozzy:**
> Do men really suffer 'shrinkage' in their private area after going swimming (especially in cold water)? If so, what sort of percentage reduction is normal – 50 per cent? More?
> Felicity, Muswell Hill

Yes, shrinkage is very real, and very upsetting. I don't know about the percentage, though: I've never thought to get out my slide rule and calculator when it's happened to me. Also, in case you're wondering, hot water *doesn't* have the reverse effect. If it did, you'd see guys walking around with electric kettles swinging from their underpants.

> **Dear Dr Ozzy:**
> I've decided I don't want any more kids, so I've asked my doc to give me the snip. Good idea?
> David, Edinburgh

There are a lot of ways to avoid having kids that don't involve surgery. Also, the thing you've gotta remember about a vasectomy is that you can't undo it – well, you *can*, but it ain't easy. I'm speaking from experience here. In the 1980s, whenever I came back from a tour, I'd get Sharon pregnant. She had our three kids – Aimee, Kelly and Jack – in three years on the trot. She'd had enough of being the size of a semi-detached house by the time Jack came along, so I went to my doc and told him to get out his sharpest pair of scissors and do what was necessary. The op was fine, although I had a bit of swelling afterwards ('Doc, can you make it *not* go away,' I said). The real problem came a few weeks later, when Sharon got all broody again. So I had to go back to the doc and ask him to unsnip me. 'I wish you lot would bloody make up your minds!' he said to me. Anyway, whatever he did to glue my tubes back together obviously didn't work, 'cos there weren't any more little Osbournes after that.

> **Dear Dr Ozzy:**
> Last month, I noticed that there seemed to be two 'balls' instead of one in my right testicle. I don't have any pain, though. Should I see my GP?
> Saif, London

Yes, *immediately*. It could be something – or it could be nothing – but if you feel any kind of strange lump in your balls, you *can't* ignore it, because it could be life-threatening. Testicular cancer is a lot more common than you'd think. A good friend of mine had it. They put some of his man-juice in a jar – in case he wanted to have kids later – got out the scissors of doom, then gave him a blast of chemo, just to be on the safe side. I'm not trying to be funny, 'cos it ain't. And I'm not saying you've got cancer, Saif. But in a case like this, don't mess around, man. Forget Dr Ozzy. Go and see a real doctor.

> **Dear Dr Ozzy:**
> I'm pretty sure I have a much smaller than average penis. As a result, I'm scared of talking to girls and am thinking of getting enlargement surgery. Is this a good idea?
> Hugh, New Mexico

Look, if it ain't broke, don't try to fix it — 'cos the only thing worse than a very small penis is a very small penis that shoots blanks and looks like some mutant fucking eel from outer space. I mean, just think of the shit that could go wrong, man. Those plastic surgeon guys couldn't even get Michael Jackson's face right, so why would you entrust them with your *dick*? I certainly wouldn't believe the e-mail ads they send out. Believe me, if that stuff really worked, there'd be lines around the block. My advice? Steer clear.

Dr Ozzy's Trivia Quiz:
Sexy Beast

*Find the answers – and add up
your score – on page 285*

1. **If your partner has a headache before sex, what's the best natural cure?**

a) A game of hide the sausage
b) An early night and plenty of sleep
c) A neck massage

2. **If a girl has a fling with a guy who says he has diphallia, what should she expect between the sheets?**

a) Delayed ejaculation
b) A 'micropenis'
c) Double the pleasure

3. **When a twenty-two-year-old student from California auctioned her virginity in 2009, how much did she get?**

a) $50,000
b) A packet of fags and a box of Maltesers
c) $3.8 million

4. **During the Honen Matsuri Festival in Japan, what do twelve men carry through the streets?**

a) A naked woman
b) An eight-foot-tall wooden schlong
c) A ceremonial bowl of human sperm

5. **A bloke in the Wodaabe tribe of Central Africa will find a wife by ...**

a) Putting on a skirt and taking part in a beauty contest
b) Arm-wrestling the potential bride's father
c) Showing the size of his woody to the town's elders

11

The Pharmacology Section

What They Don't Print on the Label

I might know fuck all about molecules, equations or the periodic table, but I do know something about chemicals – mainly 'cos I was off my nut on them for the best part of forty years. Things have changed a lot since my junkie days, though. Back in the 1970s, for example, you needed a dodgy dealer and a wad of cash to get your hands on any mind-altering substances. These days, it's all *legal*. As long as you've got a prescription, it's considered perfectly acceptable to be stoned out of your mind twenty-four hours a day, seven days a week. The problem is that people are happy to empty all these jars of pills down their necks without ever reading the labels – probably 'cos the warnings are all written by lawyers and say crazy things like: 'Side-effects might include DEATH'. That's where Dr Ozzy comes in. If you want a straight answer about a medication, why not ask someone who's taken *everything*?

Just bear in mind, before putting any drug in your body –
even if it's completely legit – you should also talk to someone who *didn't used to be in Black Sabbath*. As for all those
people who are still using illegal drugs in one way or another,
all I can say is, 'Been there, done that, and I honestly pray to
God I never go back there again.' I won't deny that some of
it was fun at the time. But so is driving your car at 150 m.p.h.
on the wrong side of the road. The trouble is, sooner or later,
there'll be an eighteen-wheeler coming round the corner in
the other direction. And that won't be any fun at all.

UPPERS

Dear Dr Ozzy:
I work at a high-energy law firm and recently got
myself a prescription for Adderall to boost my work
performance. The thing is, I'm totally not ADD. Is this
cheating at life?
Anonymous (no address given)

It really depends on how much you're taking. If you're necking a handful of the stuff at a time, then you might as well
go to work on a gram of fucking cocaine. And, as time goes
by, you'll develop a tolerance to it, and you'll have to keep
taking more and more, until you end up sitting there in your
cubicle with your eyes bugging out like a fucking nutter and
clutching at your chest every five seconds, 'cos you think
you're about to have a heart attack. That ain't cheating at
life – that's fast-tracking yourself to an early death. Personally,
I have a genuine case of ADD, but I give my Adderall to my
assistant Tony – otherwise, I'd be pouring the stuff in my

coffee and sprinkling it on my cornflakes. The fact that you're even writing to me about this suggests you know you've got a similar problem.

Dear Dr Ozzy:
I suspect that my brother has started to take cocaine when he goes out clubbing at the weekend. I'm terribly worried about him. What are the risks involved?
Susan, West Yorkshire

You're right to worry. When you start taking heavy-duty amounts of cocaine, this white gunk starts to trickle down the back of your throat, and you find yourself doing that phlegm-clearing thing all the time: like a sniff, but deeper and gunkier. And that puts a lot of stress your uvula, or 'clack', as I've always called it. When I was doing a lot of coke in the 1970s, I was clearing away phlegm so often that I ended up tearing my clack in half. I was lying in bed at the time, and I just felt it flop down in the back of my throat. Then it swelled up to the size of a golf ball and I had to go to the doc and explain myself. Luckily, he had some pills for it – but I was so paranoid from the coke, I thought I'd never sing again. So, as much fun as your brother might be having now, I'd advise him to stop while he's ahead, 'cos a coke habit never ends well.

Dear Dr Ozzy:
I recently went to Brazil and saw the most unbelievably graphic health warnings on the back of fag packets – dead babies, gangrenous feet, amputees, etc. Do you think these 'scare tactics' work or are they so over the top that they do the opposite?
Don, Greenwich

The fact that anyone can puff and cough their way through a packet of fags while staring at a picture of a foot-wide throat tumour just goes to show how addictive those fucking things are. I swear, if someone invented nicotine today, it would be in the same class as heroin – and I say that as someone who's smoked cigarettes *and* taken heroin. I remember being so hooked on tobacco, I'd pick up butts from the floor and smoke them. Disgusting, man. The thing is, though, when they start printing those horrific pictures on fag packets – like kids' corpses and whatever – you've gotta ask yourself, 'Why the hell are they selling that shit in the first place?' At some point, they've either gotta ban the things or let people get on with killing themselves.

> **Dear Dr Ozzy:**
> **My forty-six-year-old son inherited an addictive personality from his father (who was a big drinker), and has somehow ended up with a crack habit. Worse: when I went away on holiday recently, he burgled my house for drug money. I feel terrible. Why do you think he's doing this? Is it a cry for help?**
> **Jeanette, Coventry**

You answered your own question at the very beginning: no, it's not a cry for help, your son is an *addict*. He just wants his drug. It's as simple as that. A lot of people might find it hard to believe, but addiction is an illness, similar to having any other kind of mental disorder, and no one can really help you until you decide for yourself that it's time to pack it in. That ain't much comfort when the person who used to be your little angel takes up the crack pipe, though. The first thing I'd do is sit him down and tell him you know exactly what the deal is. Then give him one last chance: 'I can help you get over this, or I can let the police handle it, and you can go to prison.' If he wants your support, find a helpline or a drugs counselling service and take it from there. If he wants to be a crack-head, there ain't much you can do. At this point, tough love is the only option.

DR OZZY'S AMAZING MEDICAL MISCELLANY

Up, Up and Away

- In the 1880s, an American doc called William Halsted realised that if you shot yourself up with cocaine, it worked like an anaesthetic. Unfortunately, it also makes you a raging fucking coke-head – which is why you don't get to snort a line before having your appendix out. Halsted ended up trying to cure his own coke habit with morphine ... which just made him a coke-head *and* a smack head.

- Sigmund Freud recommended cocaine as a treatment for depression, alcoholism, morphine addiction ... and just about anything else he could think of. Mind you, coke was all the rage back then. In the 1880s you could even get bottles of 'cocaine wine' – one of the greatest inventions in the history of mankind. The drink didn't last long though, 'cos of early Prohibition laws. But they soon came up with a non-alcoholic version ... they called it 'Coca-Cola'. Six years later, the cocaine was taken out, too.

- During the Second World War, soldiers on all sides were speeding their balls off half the time – until the generals realised that there's no point being able to march three hundred miles in five minutes if you spend the next week bugging the fuck out from paranoia. If you believe some reports, even Hitler was taking methamphetamine eight times a day.

❇ Speaking of meth, in the 1940s it was approved as a treatment for everything from hay fever to narcolepsy. But it has some horrendous side-effects, including 'meth mouth', which causes your teeth to turn black and fall out. Meanwhile, to make the stuff, labs use everything from brake cleaner to laptop batteries, fertiliser, cat litter and road flares. It ain't 'organic', put it that way.

Dear Dr Ozzy:
Are energy drinks mixed with booze a safer (and legal)
alternative to cocaine?
Lizzy, London

Good question, but I don't know the answer, 'cos whenever I drank energy drinks with booze, I was on cocaine, too. As an addict, it's all the fucking same. Y'know, if people like messing themselves up, fine – but it didn't end well for me. One thing I will say is that when addicts give up the booze and the drugs, caffeine is often the only thing left for them to take. I've heard of people mixing Diet Coke and Red Bull and topping up their glass throughout the day. You see them at AA meetings, huddled around the coffee machine, twitching. It's sad, man. But the most unnatural thing for any addict is *not* to be getting high.

Anything will do. I suppose I'm lucky that I've got music to take my mind off things. And my family. And my seventeen precious dogs. And my cups of tea.

Dear Dr Ozzy:
How did you manage to quit smoking? I've tried
everything: patches, gum, cold turkey and pills, but it
isn't working for me. It's driving me insane. Please tell
me your secret – and remember, not all of us have the
money for fancy doctors!
Greg (no address given)

It's simple: you've just gotta make your mind up. I'd stop, I'd start, I'd stop again, I'd put the patch on, take the patch off, put it on again, smoke *with* the patch on, stop again, try the gum, smoke with the patch on *and* chew the gum at the same time. I even tried hypnosis at one point. I loved smoking. Cigarettes, pipes, cigars – anything. I smoked so much I set my house on fire on more than one occasion. For a while, I used to roll my own: I'd make twenty-five in one go, put them in a box, and smoke 'em through the night. I couldn't go for a walk without a cigarette, make a call without a cigarette, do *anything* without a cigarette. Then, one day, I had a conversation with myself: 'Do you really want to stop, Ozzy, or do you want to keep going? You can't do both, so make a fucking decision.' What swung it for me was the fact that I'm a singer: if I wanted to carry on entertaining people, I had to quit. So one day I went home, threw my pack on the fire, and I've never smoked since. That was eight years ago. I don't crave them any more, but every so often I'll have a twinge. I just let it go, y'know? Because I ain't under any illusions: if I have just one fag now, I'll have smoked my way through an entire packet by the end of the day.

DOWNERS

Dear Dr Ozzy:
When I drink too much, the next morning I get a super-sensitive boner. Have you ever heard of this?
Bill, Georgia

No. With the amount I used to put away, I was lucky to know I even had a dick the next morning, never mind a boner. I also had a habit of waking up in jails and hospitals, which doesn't exactly put you in the mood. The only thing that was super-sensitive was my head.

Dear Dr Ozzy:
I've recently been prescribed some medication that says 'avoid alcohol', but both my consultant and my GP say it's okay to drink 'in moderation'. They don't say what 'moderation' is, though. What's your opinion, as a man with a fair bit of experience?
Henry, Cambridgeshire

Here's my prescription for you, Henry: a new consultant and a new GP. I mean, who are these people – witch doctors? If the manufacturer of the drug goes to all the bother of putting a big yellow label on the front that says, 'AVOID ALCO-HOL', then how about *avoiding alcohol*? It ain't complicated. Y'know, sometimes I can't believe doctors. I think the problem is that they like to knock a few back themselves. I had this one bloke in London, and every time I went to his surgery, the place stank of gin, his nose glowed bright red and he chain-smoked while he scribbled down his dodgy prescriptions in a little pad. I stopped going to see him in the end – I felt worse coming out of there than I did when I went in.

> **Dear Dr Ozzy:**
> My doctor has prescribed Vicodin for a degenerative disc problem in my back, but my physical therapists say I should find an alternative to narcotics. What do you think?
> Bob, Georgia

I was hooked on that shit for a long time. Vicodin and me were made for each other – *I love it.* Especially Vicodin ES (Extra Strength). But trust me, when you're hooked on Vicodin, it's almost fucking impossible to kick. I was popping twenty-five a day at one point, and that's very dangerous, 'cos Vicodin is cut with stuff that can be extremely bad for your liver. Having said that, if you take it as your doctor prescribes it, you should be okay. So if it says, 'Take one every six hours' on the bottle, that's exactly what you've got to do. (I used to take six every hour, and blamed it on my dyslexia.) You need to work out if you trust yourself. If you decide that you don't, give the bottle to a relative or a friend, so it ain't within easy reach.

DR OZZY'S AMAZING MEDICAL MISCELLANY

Don't Get Me Down

➕ Alcohol is basically a downer, even though it can make you do crazy hyperactive shit if you drink enough of it. That's 'cos it acts in the same way as barbiturates, benzodiazepines and modern sleeping medications, like Zolpidem – reducing activity in the brain and the central nervous system.

- Barbiturates have long been used as 'truth serums' by psychiatrists and the military – mainly thanks to an American doc, William Blackwenn, who pioneered 'narcoanalysis' in the 1930s. Meanwhile, the Russians are thought to have a secret truth drug called SP-117 with no taste, no smell, no colour and no obvious side-effects.

- Mixing downers with uppers might seem like a brilliant idea at 11 p.m. on a Saturday night, but the US Food and Drug Administration doesn't agree. In 2010, it told the makers of Four Loko – nicknamed 'blackout in a can' – to stop mixing caffeine and booze. The up/down combination leaves you 'wide-awake drunk', according to some experts, meaning you don't realise how pissed you're getting. I can't help noticing that Irish coffee is still legal, though . . .

- Another downer is chloral hydrate – which became famous when a Chicago bartender, Mickey Finn, was accused of spiking his customers' drinks with it in 1903 (so he could rob 'em when they passed out). That's why, if you're drugged in a bar, it's known as being 'slipped a Mickey'. I bought some chloral hydrate myself once: it came in little gel capsules and worked a treat on overly aggressive fans.

Dear Dr Ozzy:
To numb the pain in my lower back, I've been 'chipping' with heroin – i.e., only doing it once every few days. But

I'm getting scared, because now I'm counting the hours until I can do it again. I'm not stupid: I know what smack can do to people. But I also hate people's attitudes to it. They'll skip off to the bathroom for a few lines of cocaine – just as destructive! – yet would be shocked at my smoking heroin (I don't inject). If you could give me any advice, I would very much appreciate it.
Zadie, Dublin

This ain't a good idea. I've seen the same thing happen so many times: you start 'chipping'; then the smoking becomes more regular; then, all of a sudden, it's not enough, and it leads straight to the needle. I've lost so many good friends because of that. Also, when you take street heroin – unlike an opiate that's been prescribed by a doctor – you don't know what you're getting, man. I tried street heroin twice, and it made me violently sick both times. You've also got to realise that it takes a lot of special training to administer heavy-duty pain drugs. That's why hospitals have anaesthetists. I know it can be difficult to get pills from a doctor, but if you have a genuine condition, it shouldn't be a problem. Then again, if you're anything like me, you might be using your back pain as an excuse. Either way, find a GP and/or an addiction clinic – and be honest with 'em. There's a lot of help out there, and you don't have much time to lose.

Dear Dr Ozzy:
I'm thinking of giving up booze. Does beer count?
Antony, Bristol

The first rule of alcoholism is that beer doesn't count. Neither does vodka, wine, cognac, Scotch or gin ...

Unfortunately, when you realise you don't want to be an alcoholic any more, *everything* counts. That's why you can't touch a drop. Anything else is a deal with the devil, and you'll only ever lose.

> **Dear Dr Ozzy:**
> My teenage daughter, who is half-Chinese, suffers from red flushes when she drinks alcohol – a common complaint for her ethnicity. But she says that if she takes a stomach acid tablet just before she goes out, it can be controlled. Is this dangerous, do you think?
> Anonymous, Berkshire

So, let me get this straight, Mr Anonymous from Berkshire: you're worried about the stomach acid tablet . . . but not the booze? Well, here's a little secret: I've been thrown in jail more times than I can remember; I've almost died on a number of other occasions; and I once tried to kill my own wife. And none of this happened because of Gaviscon.

> **Dear Dr Ozzy:**
> I live in Southern California and have been prescribed legal 'medical marijuana' (for muscle pain), but it's making me paranoid. How can I reduce this side-effect? And what do you think of the claimed link between pot and schizophrenia?
> Lisa, Los Angeles

When I used to smoke pot, it was happy stuff: you'd get the munchies, have a laugh and go to sleep. These days, when you have a joint, you end up holding on to your drawers and hoping you don't go insane. I don't know about the link with schizophrenia, but I do know that they fuck around with marijuana now, creating all these genetically altered mutant varieties. In the old days, a joint's level of THC – the chemical that gets you high – was something like 4 per cent. Today, you hear of it being 20 per cent or even 40 per cent. It's a bit like walking into a bar one day and being given a Bud Light, and the next day being given something that looks exactly like a Bug Light, tastes exactly like a Bud Light, but contains as much alcohol as four bottles of vodka. As for reducing your paranoia, back in the 1970s, we all thought the way to do that was to have a beer. It didn't work, though. It just made you paranoid *and* drunk.

Dear Dr Ozzy:
In your opinion, which alcoholic beverage delivers the least unpleasant hangover – red wine, vodka or beer? As the festive season approaches, I'd like to indulge in the seasonal merriment, while making the mornings after bearable.
Rod, Canterbury

Alcohol is alcohol. If you drink enough of it, nothing on the planet can save you. And after the third glass, any rule you set for yourself before you started to get slaughtered is gonna go straight out of the window anyway. So, the only thing you can really do is treat the hangover. Over the years, I developed a fail-safe cure for the morning after. I'd mix four tablespoons of brandy with four tablespoons of port, throw in some milk, a few egg yolks, and – if I was in a festive mood – some nutmeg. Then I'd down it in one gulp. It works in a very clever way: it gets you *instantly* blasted again, so you don't feel a thing. The only problem is that you've got to keep drinking *for ever* – if you don't, the hangover that eventually catches up with you is about a thousand gazillion times worse than it would have been in the first place.

> **Dear Dr Ozzy:**
> I'm a heavy boozer and now I get pains in my side quite often when I drink. I still have my appendix, both kidneys and, of course, my liver. Which organ is the problem, do you think?
> Kyle, British Columbia

I had exactly the same thing, and it turned out to be a damaged nerve from my kidneys to my liver. It was a big relief, to be honest, 'cos I was shitting myself that I had cirrhosis. I've lost many a good friend to that disease, and it ain't a pretty way to go, believe me. If you're gonna persist in drinking, my advice is to get regular blood tests, to see if your liver and kidneys are still holding up. Even better: quit. I'll never forget what happened to one guy I used to know. He was told by his doctor to stop boozing, so he went straight to the pub for his last pint, took one sip, and dropped stone dead, right there at the bar. Don't end up like him.

> **Dear Dr Ozzy:**
> I'm considering using Rohypnol – the 'date-rape drug' – as a relaxant. Is this wise?
> Catherine, Newcastle

I tried it in Germany a few years back. I'd gone to see this guy to buy some sleeping pills, but he'd sold out, so he asked if I wanted to try some Rohypnol instead. Now, as it happened, I'd heard all about it: the press was going crazy about it at the time, but I thought it was all bullshit. A drug that could completely paralyse you while you remained fully awake? It seemed too good to be true. So I bought a couple of doses of the stuff and decided to try it out in my own little science experiment. I gulped down the pills with a nip of booze as soon as I got back to my hotel room. Then I waited. 'Well, this is a load of bollocks,' I said to myself. Then, two minutes later – while I was lying on the edge of the bed, trying to order a movie on the telly with the remote control – it suddenly kicked in. I couldn't move ... *but I was wide awake!* It was the weirdest feeling, man. The only trouble was that I'd been dangling over the edge of the bed when my muscles seized up, so I ended up sliding to the floor and whacking my head on the coffee table on the way down. It hurt like fuck. I spent five hours trapped between the bed and the radiator, unable to move or talk. So I can't say I'd recommend it.

Dear Dr Ozzy:
I've been drinking heavily for a few years now, and find myself turning redder and redder. What can I do?
Jim, Devon

I looked like Rudolph the Alcoholic Fucking Reindeer by the end of my drinking days. They say blueberries can help. In my experience, though, not being off your nut twenty-four hours a day is a safer bet.

Dear Dr Ozzy:
I'm seventy-two years old and have been taking temazepam for tinnitus for a number of years (without any side-effects), but I've decided recently that I'd like

to come off the medication. I was going to go 'cold turkey', but your comments about the trouble you had coming off sleeping pills have frightened the living daylights out of me! What should I do?
Debbie, Lancaster

The most important thing to do is talk to whoever gave you the prescription. Temazepam is a very powerful drug, so don't listen to the Prince of Darkness (or anyone else) until you've heard a professional opinion. For what it's worth, it took me a year and a half to get off the stuff. And I went through *hell*. The problem is that the drug makes you used to sleeping artificially, so the withdrawal is evil. You have to do it very, *very* slowly. If you ain't having any side-effects, maybe you should ask yourself if it's really worth the trouble.

Dear Dr Ozzy:
Is it true that if you drink a pint of milk before going on the booze – to 'line your stomach' – you can avoid a hangover?
Gareth, Durham

Everyone who drinks too much has one of these ridiculous old wives' tales, but there's only one medically proven way to avoid a hangover: don't fucking drink in the first place. If you want to have a pint of milk *and* a hangover, fine, but don't kid yourself into thinking that a glass of semi-skimmed before a heavy night is gonna do you any good. That's bullshit.

Dear Dr Ozzy:
A friend of mine was hit by a car during his teens, and he's never been quite the same since. We've both

developed a taste for high-strength weed, but I've now
realised that it makes him crazy and delusional (for
instance, he says he's slept with Lady Gaga). He was
put in care for a while, but as soon as he got out he
went back to the dope. All my friends have tried telling
him to stop, but it just makes him violent. What should I
do?
Anonymous (no address given)

You can't *make* anyone do anything, but you can say to your
friend, 'Look, I'm here if you ever want my help.' I've
realised that some people can have one joint every so often
and be perfectly happy with that, and other people can't.
Personally, I started with weed and ended up on heroin. A
lot of people also make the mistake of thinking weed is
harmless, but they should ask themselves a question: if you
were gonna have open-heart surgery, and you had a choice
between a doctor who'd just smoked a couple of joints and
a doctor who'd never touched the stuff, which one would
you choose?

Dear Dr Ozzy:
Here in Denmark, people believe you can get drunk by
bathing your feet in a tub of vodka, as the skin absorbs
the booze in the same way as the lining of your
stomach. Is this true?
Henrick, Copenhagen

Yes and no. I tried it once, but got bored after a few minutes and started drinking from the foot bath. The next
morning, I wasn't sure if my feet or my mouth had given
me the hangover.

PSYCHEDELICS

Dear Dr Ozzy:
I've been taking a lot of LSD recently, mostly because
the fake reality is better than my bummer of a real life.
Have you ever felt the same way?
Anonymous (no address given)

Here's the deal, no bullshit: if you keep taking the LSD,
your 'fake reality' will soon become a lot fucking worse
than real life, no matter how bad your real life is. In my
experience, LSD is a great time until it ain't – and when
that happens, it's the worst thing that's ever happened to
you. One minute you're running down Miami Beach with
a foam finger on your head; the next, you're sticking a gun
in your best friend's face. It's worst when you want the trip
to stop, but you've still got another eight hours to go. I still
get the after-effects of LSD to this day: I call them my
'wobblers'. In a flash, every tiny little problem freaks me
out and becomes the end of the world. Seriously, man, be
very careful. If you keep taking that shit, it's gonna bite you
on the balls.

Dear Dr Ozzy:
I've heard people say LSD can cure depression. What's
your expert medical opinion on this?
Brian, Seattle

As I've said before, I wouldn't advise anyone to take acid.
On the other hand, it does open your mind to certain things.
For example, I once walked into a field in Staffordshire when

I was high on LSD and had a long conversation with a cow. After a while, the cow turned to the cow next to her and said, 'Fuck me — this bloke can *talk*.'

DR OZZY'S AMAZING MEDICAL MISCELLANY

Turn On, Tune In . . . Freak Out

➕ As crazy as it sounds, LSD is making a comeback as a legit treatment for everything from 'cluster headaches' to post-combat stress. After a forty-year ban on government-funded research, the US Food and Drug Administration is allowing trials again. LSD is still illegal and dangerous, though, so it ain't a good idea to attempt any of your own experiments.

➕ Ask any major acid-head about 'Bicycle Day' and he'll know exactly what you're talking about. This was the afternoon in 1943 when the Swiss chemist Albert Hofmann mistakenly took one hundred times the 'threshold dose' of LSD and then tried to ride home from his lab on a bicycle. Needless to say, the journey took a long time and included visits to several other universes. Before then, no one knew how high you could get on LSD (which is made from lysergic acid, found in certain fungi).

➕ No matter how much more research they do into LSD, it ain't likely to become a new blockbuster drug any time soon. All the chemical formulae behind it are now 'in the public domain', so they aren't gonna make anyone rich.

> ✚ Other common psychedelic drugs include mescaline
> (which occurs naturally in the small, spineless peyote
> cactus), psilocybin (found in certain kinds of 'magic
> mushroom') and PCP (which was used as an anaes-
> thetic until surgeons realised it made their patients
> have head-trips that were worse than their injuries).
> Illegal PCP later become known on the street as
> 'angel dust'.

Dear Dr Ozzy:
After spending the late sixties and the seventies in a
psychedelic fog, I've found that even now, after thirty
years of abstinence, my sight hasn't recovered.
Everything moves or breathes – the walls, the floors,
people's faces – and I can wake up in the night with full-
on 'acid vision'. Do you suffer from this? If so, what can
I do about it?
Phil, Aberystwyth

They used to tell you that LSD never leaves your system –
you're stuck with it for the rest of your life – although I
think that's been disproven now. It might be that something's triggering a memory of a bad trip – like when you
think about spicy food and your mouth starts to water. But
it doesn't sound very fucking normal, still having 'acid
vision' after thirty years. You should go and get an MRI
scan, because it might not have anything to do with the
crazy shit you took when you were young.

EVERYTHING ELSE

Dear Dr Ozzy:
Was Charlie Sheen really 'winning' when he was fired from *Two and a Half Men*? Or is it impossible to lead such a wild existence without some kind of tragic conclusion?
Ted, Yorkshire

There are three things I don't like discussing these days: religion, politics and Charlie Sheen. I will say this, though: if Charlie Sheen had found a cure for cancer, the guy wouldn't have got as much press as he did when he was doing his 'Winning Warlock' thing – which probably says more about our society than it does about him. Also, as a general rule, it ain't ever a good idea to make a big announcement about how you're suddenly clean and sober, 'cos you'll probably fall off the wagon at some point – and I guarantee there'll be a camera there, waiting for you. Been there, done that, got the T-shirt, the baseball cap, the mug and spoon set, and every other souvenir you can think of.

Dear Dr Ozzy:
I'm a forty-seven-year-old woman who's indulged in various medicinal herbs and chemicals for most of my life. Now I'd like to stop, but how do I fight the urge to self-medicate?
Lucille, New York

It ain't easy. When I finally admitted that I had a problem with booze, my mum said to me, 'Well, why don't you just stop bloody drinking, then?' But very few people can do that. Fortunately, there's a lot of help out there now – which wasn't the case in my day. It's good that you understand you're self-medicating, 'cos it means you ain't under any illusions, but it sounds like you haven't come to terms with the fact that you might be an addict yet. The next stage is to find a good therapist, or a local DAA group. That's how I started to get clean. Having said that, the most important thing for me was changing my social circle. I just don't hang out with practising drug addicts or alcoholics any more. When you do that, you finally realise that a case of beer and an eight-ball of cocaine for breakfast is not 'normal'.

> **Dear Dr Ozzy:**
> I'm not a big druggie, but I have a big birthday celebration coming up and I want to enjoy myself. Obviously, I don't want to cause any permanent damage – or end up in hospital – so what combination of magic plants, powders, pills and other mind-altering chemicals would you recommend for a really kick-ass time?
> **David, New York**

My favourite combination of drugs was *anything* and *anything* – and as much of both as I could get my hands on. That pretty much guaranteed a 'kick-ass time' . . . until I woke up in prison, or in the ER, or in the middle of a twelve-lane freeway. I wish I could tell you the magic formula that'll keep you out of trouble, but I never found it. Whenever I got loaded, my self-destruct circuit activated, and I ended up trying to strangle my wife, or shooting my cats, or doing some other fucked-up shit. My advice? Stay clean, man.

Dr Ozzy's Trivia Quiz:
High Expectations

*Find the answers – and add up
your score – on page 286*

1. **How can you get high from a Colorado River toad (*Bufo alvarius*)?**
a) By sucking on it
b) By milking it, drying the venom, and smoking it
c) By blending it and drinking the liquid

2. **When a British prison inmate grew a marijuana plant in his cell, what did the wardens think it was?**
a) A tomato plant
b) A Christmas tree
c) A plastic ornament

3. **When she jumped to her death from a sixth-floor window in 1969, Diane Linkletter was high on ...**
a) LSD
b) Peyote
c) Magic mushrooms

4. **When cops raided an (alleged) meth dealer's house in Mexico City, how much cash did they find hidden in the walls?**

a) $205 million
b) $25 million
c) $2 billion

5. **What was Operation Midnight Climax?**

a) A project to create an instant-orgasm pill for women
b) The secret nickname for Viagra during drug trials
c) A CIA-run brothel where the punters' drinks were spiked with LSD

12

Croaking It

Getting Ready for the Great Mosh Pit in the Sky

Knowing me, I won't leave this earth peacefully. I'll be abducted by killer turds from outer space, eaten by a giant cockroach, or crushed by a falling chunk of Halley's Comet. No matter what happens, though, one thing's for sure: my time will run out at some point. When it comes to dealing with Death, not even the Prince of Darkness gets any special favours.

It used to bother me that I wouldn't last for ever, but it doesn't any more. Don't get me wrong: I ain't planning to kick the bucket any time soon. But we're already living in an overcrowded world, and it's only gonna get worse. Then a stray asteroid will land in the ocean, some whacked-out dictator will blow up the moon, or the next Ice Age will arrive. Who wants eternal life only to see all of that bullshit happening? *Fuck that*, man: let the great-great-grandkids handle it. In the meantime, my philosophy is to make as much of what you've got for as long as is humanly possible. So, when people write to Dr Ozzy about getting old, that's what I tell 'em: accept the inevitable, but don't stop.

Never stop.

Dear Dr Ozzy:
Is it too morbid to plan your own funeral? Or is it a thoughtful gift for your surviving relatives, like when Peter Sellers asked for Glenn Miller's 'In the Mood' to be played during the service? (His final joke – everyone knew he despised the song.)
Macy, Kent

I honestly don't care what music they play at my funeral – they can put on a medley of Justin Bieber, Susan Boyle and 'We Are the Diddymen' if it makes 'em happy – but I *do* want to make sure it's a celebration, not a mope-fest. I'd also like some pranks: maybe the sound of knocking inside the coffin; or a video of me asking my doctor for a second opinion on his diagnosis. And obviously there'll be no harping on the bad times, like, 'Oh, he was terrible boozer, old Ozzy, and I'll never forget when he beat up the cat.' So, to answer your question: I do think a bit of planning is the right thing to do for the family you leave behind. Also, it's always worth remembering that a lot of people on this earth see nothing but misery their whole lives. So, by any measure, most of us in the Western world – especially rockers like me – are very lucky. That's why I don't want my funeral to be sad. I want it to be a time to say, 'Thanks.'

Dear Dr Ozzy:
I've reached the age when I need a Zimmer frame (literally). I can't begin to describe how depressing this

is. Given that you're an elder statesman of rock who still manages to be cool, can you tell me how to pull off this anti-fashion accessory? (Go-faster stripes, perhaps?)
Liv, Exeter

What do you mean, 'reached the age'? They don't say, 'Happy eighty-third birthday – here's your Zimmer frame.' My gran lived to ninety-nine without needing any help to walk. So you've obviously got a specific problem. In which case, you've gotta do what you've gotta do, man. Paint the Zimmer black and put a skull and crossbones on the front if it makes you feel better. Also, bear in mind that Johnny Cash used to ride around in a wheelchair when he got old – and he was still the coolest man on the planet.

Dear Dr Ozzy:
If you could take a test that would tell you if you're going to get Alzheimer's in the future, would you do it?
Cherry, Boston

There is a test, and Sharon and I had it done when we got our genomes sequenced (see Chapter Seven for more details). So, when the results were ready, we had to decide if we wanted to see them. It was a very big deal for Sharon, 'cos her dad had Alzheimer's, and it was horrific. Believe me, having seen what happened to him, I wouldn't wish it on my worst fucking enemy. In his heyday, my father-in-law was one of the scariest people I'd ever met, but at the end of his life he'd been reduced to a child. Having said that, my view is that if you know about something in advance, you can do a lot to slow it down. You might even have a chance of curing it, especially as new treatments come out over the years. Sharon feels the same way, so we looked at the results.

Luckily for us, nothing in our genes suggests we're any more likely to get Alzheimer's than anyone else.

> **Dear Dr Ozzy:**
> I'm approaching my eighty-fifth birthday and have now been to more friends' funerals than I care to remember. Is it better to have an early send-off or to be the last man standing?
> **Dennis, Shrewsbury**

Unless you put a gun to your head on your sixty-fifth birthday, it ain't exactly a choice you get to make, is it? Having said that, the thought of sticking around for too long seems like the worst option to me. I know a woman whose friends all died years ago, then her husband died, so she ended up living on her own. Then, to top it off, she got dementia. That ain't a life, by anyone's definition. My own mum didn't have an easy time, either. Right at the end of her life, she was robbed blind by two guys who knocked on her door and told her they were from the electricity board. I've already told my wife: if it gets to the bitter end and there's an 'off' switch you can press, don't hesitate for one second.

DR OZZY'S AMAZING MEDICAL MISCELLANY

Most Unlikely Ways to Die★

- **Hit on the head by a coconut:** Supposedly kills 150 people every year around the world, making the odds

---

★ Sources: Club Direct insurance; *101 Crazy Ways to Die* by Matt Roper; National Safety Council.

250 million to one. That means it happens more often than a fatal shark attack. Personally, I'd still rather see a coconut above my head than a fin next to me in the water.

- **Standing too close to an exploding toilet:** Self-explanatory, this one – and not exactly what you'd want anyone to write on your death certificate. It does happen, though. Estimated odds: 340 million to one.

- **Legally executed:** Obviously, this depends on which country you're in. The odds are zero in Britain, but just 97,000 to one in America.

- **Bitten by a dog:** This one's a bit of a worry, given that I've got seventeen of the fucking things. Luckily, most of 'em are the size of a tea cup. Odds: 121,000 to one.

- **Eaten by a cannibal:** How the fuck anyone calculated this statistic is beyond me, but the chances of ending up as someone's lunch allegedly works out at 25 billion to one. So, while Hannibal Lecter might scare the shit out of you, you're more likely to be hit by an asteroid (7.5 billion to one) or end your days trapped in a freezer (360 million to one).

Dear Dr Ozzy:
Suddenly, at the age of forty-three, I've found myself beginning to stutter. I'm mortified. Is this just a fact of getting older or something more serious? And is it going to get worse? Please help.
Ellen, Birmingham

It might be serious, or it might not be, but you should go and see a neurologist, just in case. I also started to jumble up my words as I got older – although stutters run in my family. It usually happens when I'm excited or frustrated. I used to treat it with a nip of booze every now and again, which helped, until I became a raging alcoholic. By the time people saw me on *The Osbournes*, they couldn't understand a word I was saying. Then I watched the show myself, and *I* couldn't understand a word I was saying. You've just got to slow down. When I stopped trying to speak fast, I stopped stuttering as much. Now, I try to think of the end of a sentence before I start it. And, although I never went to a speech therapist for my stuttering, I'm told that they can help a lot. Why not try it?

> **Dear Dr Ozzy:**
> I'm bald, fat and married, and becoming increasingly depressed by the thought that I'll never enjoy my wild days of youthful debauchery ever again. As someone who's given up drinking and philandering, how do you come to terms with getting old?
> **Mike, New Jersey**

Whatever you do, *don't* just sit there like a lump, waiting for the Grim Reaper to arrive. Find something you enjoy doing, maybe some kind of exercise – although *not* bonking the next-door neighbour's wife – and let off your pent-up frustration through that. Look at me: I'm sixty-two years old, I don't drink, I don't smoke, and I don't run around with groupies any more, but I'm still doing a two-and-a-half-hour rock'n'roll show in a different city every night, and – in my head at least – I feel like I'm twenty-one. Don't give up, man. Accept the things you can't change and get on with your life.

DR OZZY'S AMAZING MEDICAL MISCELLANY

Most Likely Ways to Die*

⊞ A mind-blowing 59 million people (roughly) die every year on Planet Earth, with the most common cause being a dodgy ticker. Heart disease accounts for 12.2 per cent of all deaths throughout the world.

⊞ Strokes give heart attacks a good run for their money on the Grim Reaper's Hit List, coming in at number two and killing 5.7 million people annually – 9.7 per cent of all deaths.

⊞ Pneumonia and emphysema (or lower respiratory infections and chronic obstructive pulmonary disease, to use the proper terms) come in at numbers three and four. Unsurprisingly, smoking fags is the leading cause of emphysema – another very fucking good reason to quit.

⊞ Never in a billion years would I have guessed the fifth most common cause of death in the world. It's diarrhoea. Tragically, more than half of all the 2.2 million victims each year are kids under the age of five. Although it's easily treatable in the West, if you're in a poor country a bad case of the runs can kill you through dehydration and fluid loss – especially if you're already malnourished.

⊞ The other most common ways to die are: AIDS (number six), tuberculosis (number seven), lung cancer (number eight), road traffic accidents (number nine) and premature birth/low birth weight (number ten).

---

* Source: World Health Organisation.

Dear Dr Ozzy:
As the Prince of Darkness, are you a supporter of the
American euthanasia advocate Jack Kevorkian – a.k.a.
'Dr Death' – who spent almost a decade in prison?
Carlos (no address given)

To a certain degree, I understood why Dr Death said that
doctors should be able to help their patients top themselves. Then again, knowing America the way I do, if
it became legal, somebody would end up doing a deal –
'If you pop my nan, I'll give you a quarter of the inher-
itance,' that kind of thing. Some of the doctors here –
and anywhere else, probably – would kill you for ten
grand, no problem at all. You'd also have elderly relatives
feeling pressured into taking the death juice, 'cos they
wouldn't want to 'be a burden', y'know? So I'd at least
want there to be some kind of process – not just 'Squeeze
this trigger and you're gone. See ya'. Having said that,
though, I've always told Sharon, 'If my quality of life
is terrible, if I can't go for a piss by myself, if I'm paral-
ysed – you have my permission to pull the plug.' Some
people might say, 'That's going against God,' but getting
medical treatment is going against God, too, isn't it? If
you've got a headache, it certainly ain't God who hands
over the aspirin.

Dear Dr Ozzy:
At sixty-two, you are so good looking, man! What is
your secret? Have you got some kind of magic shake
that gives you eternal youth? Could you share this
formula with us?
Klausitta, Tallinn

It's called English breakfast tea, with a good brand of honey. I get through about ten bowls of that stuff a day. I also eat as much fruit as I can. Forget bowls of brown M&Ms: the first thing I ask for when I go to any hotel room on the road is a selection of the local fruit. They also say that alcohol preserves ... but I don't believe that for one fucking second.

DR OZZY'S INSANE-BUT-TRUE STORIES

The Age of the Supercentenarian

➕ When I was a kid, people counted themselves lucky if they lived long enough to get a gold watch and a retirement bash down at the pub. Nowadays, you can be retired for longer than you ever worked. Take Jeanne Calment, the French woman who broke the record for the longest (independently verified) human lifespan. She was born in 1875 in Arles and managed to outlive her entire family, including her grandson (he died in 1963 when he fell off a motorbike). She was so old, she'd even met Vincent van Gogh – although she thought he was a c***. ('Dirty, badly dressed, disagreeable ... very ugly, ungracious, impolite [and] sick,' she told an interviewer.) She was a remarkable woman: she took up fencing at the age of 85; kept riding a bicycle until she was 100; and smoked fags every day until she was 117. Meanwhile, she never went on a diet, and never stopped eating her two favourite things: olive oil and chocolate. She finally passed away in 1997, at the age of 122 years and 164 days. People who live beyond the age of 110 are now known as 'supercentenarians', and there are between 300 and 450 of 'em around the world today. But that number's sure to rise over the next few years.

Dear Wonderful Doctor of Oz:
Now that I'm getting older, my feet constantly burn after a long day at work. I go home and rub them for two hours, but they still ache. I'd like to hope that this isn't just the reality of age. Have you ever had achy breaky feet? (Please don't say that I need feet transplants.)
Dusty, Coventry

There's an easy cure for this, Dusty: learn to walk on your hands. Give it a week, and the pain will be gone. Promise.

Dear Dr Ozzy:
I'm getting to the age when I need to have my first prostate check-up. Do you recommend the 'digital rectal exam' or can I get away with the (less intrusive) urine screening test?
Christian, Stoke Newington

I don't care if it's a blood test, a urine test or if they have to stick a bicycle frame up there – *get it done.* I've lost too many friends to prostate cancer to worry about any temporary discomfort.

Dear Dr Ozzy:
My ninety-two-year-old mother is becoming unbearable. She's in good enough shape to live by

herself but relies on me for almost 24/7 support,
making it impossible for me to enjoy my retirement
with my husband while we're still both in good health.
Even if we go away for a weekend, she calls day and
night, laying on the emotional blackmail. What can I
do?
Anne, Cumbria

Here's the problem with hanging on to your marbles for so long: you end up becoming very aware of how difficult, lonely and painful your life is getting – and it doesn't put you in a very good mood. I've personally never had to deal with that kind of situation, 'cos both my parents died quite young, and my father-in-law had Alzheimer's, which meant he didn't have a clue what time of day it was. As heavy duty as Alzheimer's is, I sometimes wonder if that's the better way to go. But, y'know, there's no getting away from the fact that modern medicine has created a whole new set of issues when it comes to people living to these crazy ages – and I don't think we're anywhere near getting to the bottom of them. My only advice is to go to your doctor, tell them that this situation is gonna send you to the loony bin, and find out what kind of help might be available. Even if you have to pay for a private nurse out of your own pocket, it might be worth it. As you say, *you* ain't gonna live for ever, either.

Dr Ozzy's Trivia Quiz:
Meet the Worms

*Find the answers – and add up
your score – on page 00*

1. **For a fee, a US company will turn your cremated remains into ...**

a) Stained glass

b) A salad bowl (with optional tongs)

c) A diamond

2. **What is a 'sky burial'?**

a) When your ashes are blasted into outer space on a Russian-made rocket

b) When your corpse is fed to vultures

c) When your ashes are thrown out of a plane over your favourite place

3. **Which of these last will and testaments is real?**

a) The Australian bloke who left one shilling to his wife – 'for a tram fare so she can go somewhere and drown herself'

b) The Beverly Hills socialite who asked to be buried in her Ferrari, wearing a lace gown, 'with the seat slanted comfortably'

c) The countess who left $80 million to her dog

4. **What did Duke Ferdinand of Brunswick demand to have in his coffin?**

a) A window
b) An air tube
c) A lid he could unlock and open from the inside – allowing him to walk out into his tomb if he 'woke up' (with the key to be put in his shroud pocket)

5. **'Angel lust' is what, exactly?**

a) When a corpse gets a boner
b) When someone wishes for an early death
c) When someone turns religious on their death bed

Dr Ozzy's Prescription Pad

Take as Directed . . .

As much as this book ain't supposed to be taken too seriously, I hope you've learned a few things along the way. I know *I* have. When people ask you for advice every week, it's liking getting a crash course in human nature. You also learn a lot about yourself . . . in a weird kind of way. So, before I sign off, here are a ten simple tips for living a long and happy life that I've come up with during my time as Dr Ozzy. They won't solve *every* problem. But if you keep 'em in mind, you'll at least have a shot at avoiding some of the stupid fucking mistakes I've made over the years.

God bless you all.

- Your doctor has seen patients come through his door with fluorescent green dicks and/or family pets stuck up their arseholes. So, trust me, whatever's wrong with you ain't as embarrassing as you think it is.
- If you think it might be the booze, *it's the booze.*

- No one's family is perfect. Worry about *real* problems, not about what other people think.
- If you find a lump – *any* lump – don't prick it with a pin, hit it with a mallet, look it up on the internet, or ask Dr Ozzy if you should wait until it grows into a second head. Get it checked out, *now*. (And get a physical every year, too.)
- Your genes don't decide who you are – *you* do. If the Prince of Darkness managed to get clean and sober after forty years of over-indulgence, *anything* is fucking possible.
- People who make you feel bad about yourself ain't your real friends.
- Most of us are fucking lunatics, one way or another. Some just hide it better than others.
- If you write to Dr Ozzy to ask if something is right or wrong, you already know it's wrong.
- All drugs are basically the same – booze, pot, cocaine, heroin … whatever. They're just different ways to escape from life. So, before asking if 'a little bit' of this or that is safe in moderation, here's my answer: do it if you want to, man, but don't kid yourself. You certainly ain't kidding anyone else.
- *Always* get a second opinion – even if that means calling your doctor on a mobile from six feet under to ask him if he's 100 per cent sure you're dead.

Dr Ozzy's advice column appears every week in the *Sunday Times* and in select issues of *Rolling Stone*.

Write to Dr Ozzy at: **AskDrOzzy@Sunday-Times.co.uk**

Quiz Answers

Award yourself one point for each correct answer, add up your total, then see how you did on page 289.

Magic Medicines

1. b). I ain't kidding – you can even look up the article in the *British Medical Journal* online. The scientists said they wanted 'to assess the effects of didgeridoo playing on daytime sleepiness ... by reducing collapsibility of the upper airways in patients with moderate obstructive sleep apnoea syndrome and snoring'. And I thought my job was fucking ridiculous.
2. a). They turn the poor old frog into juice by dropping it in a blender (they kill it and skin it first). They also spice it up with 'white bean broth', honey, raw aloe vera and maca (an Andean root). If throwing up gives you a raging boner, it probably works a treat.
3. c). Makes sense, I suppose, 'cos bats have amazing night vision. Still, as one of the few people on this planet who have actually swallowed bat's blood, I can tell you that it doesn't have any special powers – otherwise I wouldn't have needed eye surgery in 2010.

4. a). This a terrible myth, 'cos it's been used to justify rape, and it makes the disease spread much faster.
5. b). Not much of a surprise, this one. In the 1960s everyone tried to cure everything with LSD.

Health Nut

1. a). They call it 'fat' for a reason. One tablespoon of the stuff has about 120 calories, compared with 112 for ghee, and 101 for butter (according to Nutrientfacts.com and Fitday.com).
2. All three. Or at least that's the advice of a weird-sounding organisation called the National Digestive Diseases Information Clearinghouse (NDDIC). It also says you will swallow less air if you eat your meals slower and make sure your false choppers fit right.
3. a). The poor fucker who did the fieldwork to come up with this number deserves the Victoria Cross, if you ask me (he works for the NDDIC). But thank God this kind of information exists, 'cos next time I'm feeling intimidated by someone, I'll remind myself that they burped or let their arse cheeks blow fourteen times in the previous twenty-four hours.
4. b) and c). If you overdo it when you're training, you can end up feeling like you're wading through molten lead. When that happens, you've gotta slow down and see a doc, or you might do yourself some serious damage. Pregnant women and overweight people can also get heavy legs – as can anyone who stands or sits in the same position for too long.
5. b). The guy was tough as nails – he never even warmed up before exercising. 'Does a lion warm up when he's

hungry?' he once said. 'No! He just goes out there and eats the sucker.' (Nevertheless, Dr Ozzy recommends frequent stretching.)

Being Beautiful

1. a) and b). If you believe what you read on the internet, Cleopatra also used crocodile turds as a contraceptive. Hence the old Egyptian chat-up line, 'Wanna come back to my place and see my dung?'
2. All three. They were recommended as baldness cures for Julius Caesar, who also tried to compensate for his thinning rug by buying himself a red convertible chariot.
3. c). Generally speaking, if your car windows don't have special UV-protection, they'll block most UVB rays – which tan and burn you the most – but not UVA rays, which give you wrinkles and cause so-called 'commuter ageing'.
4. c). The Sultan of Brunei (according to the *Sunday Times*). He flew his barber from the Dorchester Hotel in Mayfair to Brunei (7,000 miles) and paid for a private suite on Singapore Airlines to make sure he didn't catch swine flu on the way. Seems perfectly sensible to me.
5. a). Which shouldn't exactly come as a fucking surprise if you've ever been to the Czech Republic. The first 'beer spa' opened at a brewery in Chodovz Plana, near Prague, in 2006.

Flesh & Blood

1. b). His brothers did it 'cos they were jealous. They also nicked his coat and him threw down a mine shaft. They didn't let him play with their X-Box, either.

2. c). The mother was supposedly a Russian peasant, married to a guy named Feodor Vassilyev (her first name has been lost to history). According to the *Guinness Book of Records*, she pumped out sixteen pairs of twins, seven sets of triplets, and four sets of quadruplets between 1725 and 1765. Only two of the babies died in infancy. Feodor – otherwise known as the Man with the Golden Balls – went on to remarry and have another twenty kids.

3. a). According to news reports, the victim (who wasn't named) didn't realise what had happened until she noticed a wet feeling under her shirt, pulled it up, and saw her nipple fall to the floor. She put it in a bag and took it to hospital. It's now back where it belongs.

4. c). 'Marriage should be about losing arguments and winning relationships,' according to Rabbi Shmuley Boteach, a leading relationship coach.

5. c). Lina Medina's parents took her to hospital, thinking she had a stomach tumour. It turned out she was seven months pregnant. She's now in her seventies and lives in Peru. Lina was able to have a kid so young because of her very unusual case of 'precocious puberty' – her first period arrived when she was a toddler. Although, of course, it's beyond tragic that some scumbag (he was never identified) then impregnated her. The baby was raised as Lina's brother and died in 1979, at the age of forty.

Under the Knife

1. a) and c). The guy with the forked tongue – Erik Sprague – had it done on purpose, 'cos he wanted to look like a lizard. He had his teeth filed into fangs, too. He's available for babysitting duties.

2. a) and c). The woman who injected lubricant into her face told *ABC News*: 'By the following day [my whole face] was just completely inflamed. [The lubricant] expands, it's like rubber, and your own collagen forms scar tissue around it . . . It looked like horrible blisters.' People who do this kind of thing to themselves suffer from a condition called body dysmorphic disorder – which means they drive themselves nuts about one particular part of their body, to the point where they're willing to self-operate.

3. b). The *Annals of General Psychiatry* says that 'severe intentional eye self-injury is uncommon, but not rare' and that it's usually a result of a drug freak-out psychosis, bipolar disorder, obsessive compulsive disorder, post-traumatic stress disorder, and/or depression. Some patients have been found with a copy of the passage in Matthew's Gospel, which says, 'if the right eye offends thee, pluck it out and cast it from thee'.

4. a). They were known as 'barber surgeons'. The most common service they provided was 'bloodletting' – where they cut a gash in your arm and let your blood run into a bucket. Personally, I'd have been happy with a short back and sides.

5. a). The poor guy, who was seventy years old and mentally ill, died from septicaemia within six days. The others are real cases that have appeared in *The Psychiatrist,*

although the bright spark with the bicycle got it wrong
and ended up fracturing his skull instead.

Doctor! Doctor!

1. a). He was sacked and fined for making out prescriptions to himself, then booked himself into rehab. He
   wasn't struck off, though – and went on to kill over two
   hundred patients, that we know of, at least.
2. a). The woman later withdrew her accusation and the
   doc was exonerated.
3. b). He allegedly told one woman that his magic
   potion would stop her gums bleeding, but warned her
   that it might 'taste funny'. He also told her she could
   swallow it if she wanted to. He might be getting similar treatment himself now that he's in jail.
4. c). 'I hope that what I've done will reassure men that
   vasectomies can be relatively pain free,' he told the
   BBC. He added that he'd been thinking of getting the
   snip for a while, but wanted someone trustworthy to do
   it. 'Eventually, I just thought, sod it, I'll do it myself,' he
   said.
5. c). A 2010 Gallup poll revealed just how much dough
   gets spent on 'defensive medicine' – basically, doctors
   covering their own arses in case a patient tries to take
   'em to the cleaners.

Mutant Strains

1. a). When the bones of tiny, hobbit-like creatures were
   found on a remote Indonesian island, Flores, some

scientists thought they might have been humans with a crazy genetic disorder who lived 18,000 years ago. Others said they were an entirely different species.

2. a) and b). Although it looked like she had four arms and four legs, she was actually *two* people. After a mind-blowing twenty-seven-hour operation, little Lakshmi – who was worshipped as a Hindu goddess by some Indians – now goes to school and can walk on her own. The poor kid still needs more surgery, though.

3. a) I almost fell out of my fucking chair when I heard about this. It ain't the antifreeze you put in your car, mind you, but an 'antifreeze protein' found in certain Antarctic fish that stops 'em dying from the cold. They've even started to use the stuff in low-fat ice cream – although it's grown in a lab, not taken directly out of some smelly old flounder.

4. c). An Austrian monk called Gregor Mendel had the mega-brainwave that led to modern genetics after growing and studying 29,000 pea plants between 1856 and 1863. He didn't get any recognition during his lifetime. On the upside, he never went hungry in the lab.

5. b). One of the scientists who cloned her said, 'Dolly is derived from a mammary gland cell, and we couldn't think of a more impressive pair of glands than Dolly Parton's!'

Personal Skills

1. c). I'm told the other two greetings work in Oman (nose kiss) and some parts of Niger ('*Whooshay!*'). But

always double-check before giving a stranger a smacker on the conk, no matter where you are.

2. c). 'Don't put your phone on the dining table, or glance at it longingly mid-conversation,' they say. Other mobile rules include: don't make calls from the shitter; don't have phone conversations in public about money, sex or your latest haemorrhoid attack; and think carefully before choosing 'My Humps' as a ringtone.

3. a). Not that I'd know – I don't have the first fucking clue about computers. And experts say that the human brain can handle a maximum number of 150 *real* friends, so if you've got more than that, you might want to take advantage of National Unfriend Day (17 November).

4. b). During the heist – which the boss had helped to plan – his employees were held at knifepoint and one teller was punched in the face. The boss pretended to be a hostage until the cops showed up and realised that one of the masked robbers was his girlfriend.

5. a). 'There were problems with money in the workplace and basically the stress of him being the owner and running a business got to him,' said the cops.

Grey Matter

1. All of them: a) is also known as 'muscle dysmorphia', 'cos suffers never think they look 'ripped' enough; b) is usually caused by a major brain injury; and c) is described by experts as an 'exaggerated startle reflex' – in other words, you pretty much crap your pants whenever you're surprised. Weirdly, it was first discovered among French-speaking lumberjacks living in Maine, USA.

2. a). It means you're turned on by people who commit crimes. It's also known as 'Bonnie and Clyde syndrome'.

3. a). I ain't exactly a brain surgeon, but I'm told that this is more or less true (apparently, headaches come from blood vessels, the membrane around the brain and other nerves). If you're ever unlucky enough to have brain surgery, you can even get away with just a local anaesthetic on your scalp. As for the other two: at most, your brain could power only a 23-watt bulb; and the biggest emotional memory trigger is thought to be smell.

4. b). That's what the scientist Stephen Juan said in his 1998 book *The Odd Brain*. Most thoughts are turned into very short-term memories and then forgotten. Make that 'all thoughts' in my case.

5. c). That makes 'em the second most commonly prescribed drugs in the country – after high blood pressure medication (according to a 2005 report from the Centers for Disease Control and Prevention).

Sexy Beast

1. a). The serotonin released when you bonk is like nature's aspirin, according to Dr Vincent Martin – who was recently voted the Best Doctor in the World by married men everywhere.

2. c). Diphallia means you're born with two dicks (one is usually bigger than the other). It ain't exactly common, though: there have been only 100 cases since the first one was recorded in 1609.

3. c). The 'buyer' – a thirty-eight-year-old Australian

businessman, if you believe what you read in the papers – backed out at the last minute . . . 'cos his wife found out. It still ain't clear if he got his $250,000 deposit back. The whole thing was a PR stunt organised by a knocking shop in Nevada.

4. b). The festival is held every year on 15 March – and everyone gets blasted on sake. The guys who carry the giant dick have to be exactly forty-two years old, 'cos it's believed to be an unlucky age.

5. a). The beauty contest is known as the Gerewol and happens every September, with the guys trying to show off their height and the whiteness of their eyes and teeth. As if that weren't freaky enough, they also get out of their minds on a drink made of psychoactive bark.

High Expectations

1. b). If you milk the venom and dry it out, you end up with a drug called bufotenine, which – when smoked – gives the same kind of high as LSD. Don't try it, though, 'cos it's illegal (and the toads are endangered). A former Scout leader in California is one of the few people who've ever been arrested for taking a 'toad trip'. He told agents that his mind was blown so wide open, he could 'hear electrons jumping orbitals in my molecules'.

2. a) and b). The criminal managed to grow the pot plant for five months at Verne Prison in Dorset – he even hung tinsel on it over Christmas – before the screws finally realised that the mile-wide grin on his face wasn't due to the bracing sea air.

3. None of 'em, according to the autopsy. But her dad, the TV presenter Art Linkletter, blamed a flashback from LSD – which led to the theory that people think they can fly when they're freaking out on acid.

4. a). They also found 'eight luxury vehicles, seven weapons, and a machine to make pills'. The alleged dealer, a Chinese guy, was later arrested in the US.

5. c). It was part of the CIA's crazy MK-Ultra mind-control programme in the 1950s and 1960s. Punters were lured into a brothel in San Francisco, then drugged and sexually blackmailed while agents sat behind two-way glass, taking notes. The CIA thought the Johns would be too embarrassed to complain to the cops the next morning. They were right.

Meet the Worms

1. c). LifeGem takes carbon from human remains and uses it to make synthetic diamonds. In 2007, the company made a diamond partly from carbon extracted from ten strands of Ludwig van Beethoven's hair. It sold on eBay for $202,700 (the money went to charity).

2. b). Tibetans used to do this 'cos most of 'em are Buddhists and think the human body is an 'empty vessel' after death. Also, Tibet is a rocky place, so digging graves ain't easy – and cremation would use up scarce firewood. There are some crazy pictures on the internet of 'body-breakers' cutting up corpses while the vultures queue up for their dinner.

3. All of 'em. The socialite was Sandra Ilene West, who died at thirty-seven from a drug overdose. The car – a powder-blue 1964 Ferrari 330 'America' – was put in

a wooden box, covered with concrete (to make sure no one would nick it) and lowered into a hole in the Alamo Masonic Cemetery in Texas. For organising the burial, her brother-in-law was given a $2 million inheritance. If he'd refused to do it, he would have got only $10,000.

4. All three of 'em. This happened in the 1700s, when 'safety coffins' were all the rage after a few horrendous cases of people being buried alive. Other coffin designs had cords attached to church bells, so you could sound the alarm if you 'woke up'. The only problem was that bodies usually swell up and move as they decompose, so sometimes a fresh corpse in the churchyard would ring the bell, scaring the shit out of the vicar.

5. a). A 'death erection' usually happens after being hanged, shot in the head or poisoned (it's technically known as a 'priapism', and you can also get it after suffering a severe spinal cord injury, I'm told). If Mother Nature had any mercy, she'd give you the boner *before* you died.

HOW DID YOU SCORE?

41–60: Medical genius. If you haven't tried brain surgery yet, now might be the time.

21–40: Hypochondriac. You have just enough knowledge to be a danger to yourself and society.

0–20: Medical liability. You're so clueless, you could end up accidentally stabbing yourself in the kidney while clipping your toenails. Wear Bubble-Wrap and remain indoors at all times.